The Great Deceiver

THE GREAT DECEIVER

Seeing Satan for What He Is

Paul W. Powell

BROADMAN PRESS
Nashville, Tennessee

© Copyright 1988 • Broadman Press
All rights reserved
4219-57

ISBN: 0-8054-1957-8

Dewey Decimal Classification: 235.47
Subject Heading: DEVIL
Library of Congress Catalog Card Number: 87-17363
Printed in the United States of America

Unless otherwise stated, Scripture quotations are from the King James Version of the Bible. Scripture quotations marked (NASB) are from the *New American Standard Bible.* Copyright © The Lockman Foundation, 1960, 1962, 1963, 1968, 1971, 1972, 1973, 1975, 1977. Used by permission. Scripture quotations marked (Phillips) are reprinted with permission of Macmillan Publishing Co., Inc. from J. B. Phillips: *The New Testament in Modern English,* Revised Edition. © J. B. Phillips 1958, 1960, 1972. Scripture quotations marked (RSV) are from the Revised Standard Version of the Bible, copyrighted 1946, 1952, © 1971, 1973. Scripture quotations marked (TLB) are from *The Living Bible.* Copyright © Tyndale House Publishers, Wheaton, Illinois, 1971. Used by permission.

Library of Congress Cataloging-in-Publication Data

Powell, Paul W.
   The Great Deceiver / Paul W. Powell.
   p.   cm.
   Bibliography: p.
   ISBN 0-8054-1957-8 (pbk.)
   1. Devil. I. Title.
BT981.P68 1988
235'.47—dc 19   87-17363
                                                                                            CIP

Introduction

Winston Churchill once said of Kaiser Wilhelm that he wanted to be a Napoleon without fighting Napoleon's battles; the Kaiser wanted victories without wars.

Don't we all? Especially in the Christin life. But it is just not possible. There are no victories without battles.

It is a great mistake to think that at the happy hour of our conversion all trouble and strife cease. In reality that hour marks the beginning of a lifelong warfare—not a war for our salvation, to be sure, but a war in Christian service.

That's what this book is all about: winning at the Christian warfare. It presents Satan as the opponent of God and His people and shows how Satan and his vast demonic forces work to thwart the purposes of God and His church in today's world.

"Why," I hear someone say, "why talk about this kind of thing? Why don't you talk about something more relevant? Why don't you Christians get busy and do something that is meaningful today?"

But what could be more relevant than teaching that puts its finger on the basic problem of the world? What good is it to keep rushing around curing fevers but never stopping to analyze the disease? This is what the world does. It puts Band-Aids on cancers.

There is a serious disease at work in the human race, and it is constantly breaking out in little fevers, but we are content to give aspirin for the fever, never once inquiring what the diseases.

We must learn how the devil works, but, more than that, we must learn the process of conquering him—not by flesh and blood, not by joining committees or new activities. Our weapons are not carnal, but spiritual, not of the body.

This is the amazing truth we must learn: God has made full provision for us to fight these great and powerful forces which hold the world in their grip.

This is a book for these times. It presents the Bible view of the subject of Satan and the forces at his command. At the same time it shows how Christians are on the victor's side, that we are "more than conquerors through him that loved us" (Rom 8:37). The theme of this book is how Christians may lay hold of this victory and make it actual in everyday experience.

Here is no armchair theory, but practical instruction based on the teachings of the Word of God and tested in the daily conflicts that arise from the evil spirits arrayed against us. How good it is to learn that so great is God's provision in Christ that the believer may be victorious in every encounter with Satan and the forces of evil.

Contents

1. Like a Roaring Lion 9
2. Born-Again Christians with Birth Defects 21
3. The God of This World 31
4. The Battle for the Mind 41
5. The Devil's Blockades 51
6. The Messenger of Satan 61
7. An Angel of Light 71
8. The Device of Divisiveness 85
9. The Binding of Satan 97
10. Victors Instead of Victims 107
11. Seven Secrets to Starting Over 119
12. The Downfall of the Great Deceiver 131

1

Like a Roaring Lion

Sir Edward Creasy in his exciting book, *Fifteen Decisive Battles of the World,* lists Gettysburg, Stalingrad, and the Battle of Britain. But beyond these battles is the most important of all—the Christian's warfare.

When we become Christians, we enter into spiritual conflict. The enemy is Satan, the battleground is our mind, and the issue is our Christian walk. We do not live in a neutral world. There are hostile forces at work in it, an evil one with a host of helpers opposed to God and to man.

The war began in heaven! "There was war in heaven: Michael and his angels fought against the dragon; and the dragon fought and his angels. And the great dragon was cast out . . . into the earth, and his angels were cast out with him" (Rev. 12:7,9). Today the battle has shifted from heaven to earth and rages both around us and in us.

Paul spoke of the Christian warfare when he wrote:

> Finally, my brethren, be strong in the Lord, and in the power of his might. Put on the whole armour of God, that ye may be able to stand against the wiles of the devil. For we wrestle not against flesh and blood, but against principalities, against powers, against the rulers of the darkness of this world, against spiritual wickedness in high places (Eph. 6:10-12).

This analogy of the Christian as a soldier is a very popular one in the New Testament.

The apostle Peter dealt with our spiritual struggle when he wrote, "Be sober, be vigilant; because your adversary the devil, as a roaring lion, walketh about, seeking whom he may devour: Whom resist stedfast in the faith" (1 Pet. 5:8-9).

The word *adversary* is a legal term that describes an opponent in a court of law. The first time I saw that word used in this sense was in Belize, Central America. The sign in front of a lawyer's office read, "John Smith, Adversary at Law." In the Greek the word originally meant "anyone who puts himself hostile toward another." Through the years it has come to designate an enemy.

All believers have a spiritual enemy called the devil or Satan with whom they must contend. The Christian life is not a Sunday School picnic or an afternoon stroll through the park. It is an all-out war against an unseen enemy. An evil person in the world is in deadly conflict with both God and man.

You might be thinking, *Surely, you don't believe in a real devil, horns, red suit and all, do you?* No, I don't believe in the red suit and horns, but I do believe in him. Like Charles G. Finney, I believe in the devil for two reasons: first because the Bible says so and second because I've done business with him before.

Robert Louis Stevenson said "You know the Caledonian Railway Station in Edinburgh? One cold, east windy morning I met Satan there." Everyone knows the kind of experience of which Stevenson spoke.

The Bible most certainly speaks of Satan—over a hundred and seventy-seven times in all. I have had multiple personal encounters with him. Yes, I believe in the devil. He's real.

When I hear someone question the reality of Satan, I think about the bruised and bleeding boxer who went to his corner after a bad round. His trainer splashed cold water on his head and rubbed him down as his manager tried to encourage him. He said, "Rocky, you are doing great. Your opponent hasn't laid a glove on you."

The half-dazed boxer looked up and said, "If my opponent hasn't laid a hand on me, you'd better keep an eye on that referee because somebody out there is beating the daylights out of me."

If the devil isn't real, someone else like him is continually assaulting me. How else can we explain the demonic in the human heart? How else can we account for the reality and the extent of evil in the world? Not to believe in Satan is to blame God for all.

Our sophisticated age is prone to deny the devil's existence, to ignore him, or to make jokes about him. But he is real and at work, and nothing delights him more than our not thinking so.

The Bible never tries to prove Satan's existence. What the Scriptures do is identify the source of temptation and evil. We know that it is there. We have felt it pull us like a magnet, but we do not know its source apart from God's Word. The Bible identifies temptation as coming from Satan.

To be successful in spiritual warfare, we need to know our enemy. To this end consider these five questions: (1) Who is our adversary? (2) What is he like? (3) Where did he come from? (4) Why does God allow him to exist? (5) How can we defeat him?

The False Accuser

Who is our adversary? He is called by many names in Scripture. He is called Lucifer, the shining one. He is called Satan, the slanderer. He is called Beelzebub, lord of flies. In 1 Peter 5:8 he is called the devil. The Greek word for *devil* is *diabolos* which means "false accuser." He is the one who falsely accuses and attempts to separate man from man and man from God by slandering both man and God.

The first time we meet the adversary in Scripture he is involved in false accusations. The Book of Genesis opens with God placing man in the beautiful Garden of Eden and giving him the run of the place. Man is forbidden to do only one thing—eat the fruit of the tree of the knowledge of good and evil. God warned, "The day that thou eatest thereof thou shalt surely die" (Gen. 2:17).

Satan appeared, accused God of lying, and said to Eve, "Ye shall not surely die: For God doth know that in the day you eat thereof, then your eyes shall be opened, and you shall be as gods, knowing good and evil" (Gen. 3:4-5). Satan's purpose was to discredit God by falsely accusing Him of deceit.

When we meet Satan again in the Book of Job, he is doing the same thing. Job was a godly man who served the Lord with a sincere heart. Satan appeared before God and accused Job of having a fair-weather faith. He insinuated that Job served God for mercenary reasons only and that if Job's good life were interrupted his faith would melt away. Satan cast a question mark over the character of this good man. He slandered him before God.

Satan is always doing that. John, in the Revelation, described him as "the accuser of our brethren . . . which accused them before our God night and day" (12:10).

Let me show you how Satan operates. He is the author of sickness, disease, and tragedy. He is the one behind the suffering and sorrow of our world. But when have you ever heard of a person diagnosed as having cancer asking,

"Why has Satan done this to me?" People are always labeling these things as "acts of God." They ask, "Why has God done this to me?"

Do you see how subtle Satan is? He brings havoc to the world, and God gets blamed for it. He is the one who hurts people, and God is discredited because of it.

Satan deceived Adam and Eve (Gen. 3). *Satan* stood against Israel (1 Chron. 21:1). *Satan* afflicted Job (Job 1:1-2). *Satan* tempted Jesus (Matt. 4:10). *Satan* infilled Judas (Luke 22:3). *Satan* sifted Peter (Luke 22:31). *Satan* hindered Paul (1 Thess. 2:18). *Satan* deceives the whole world (Rev. 12:9).

He is the one who opposes and obstructs. He is determined to rob God of His right to rule in the hearts and lives of men, and he is determined to rob man of the privilege of living in heaven. He is the enemy of God and of man. In the Scriptures there is just one *diabolos*—Satan, the sovereign ruler over all the demons of darkness, despair, and destruction. However, there is a vast demonic force under his rule.

Created, not Born

Where did Satan come from? That's a fair question. Most of us would like to know. The answer to it is not easy, however. The origin of Satan is shrouded in mystery.

The Bible does not give us a clear picture regarding Satan's beginning. He just appears on the stage of divine history as a created being, a rebel against God.

Apparently Satan is a fallen angel. Peter spoke of the "angels that sinned" (2 Pet. 2:4) and Jude of the "angels which kept not their first estate" (Jude 6). Jesus Himself spoke of Satan, fallen like lightning from heaven (Luke 10:18*b*).

What happened? Two passages in the Bible seem to cast

light on this: Ezekiel 28:11-19 and Isaiah 14:12-17. According to Isaiah, Satan's original name was Lucifer, "the shining one." Ezekiel called him "brightness," which can be translated Lucifer. He was the chief of all angels. In his exalted position he let pride get the best of him. He started thinking of his beauty and his wisdom as something he had achieved rather than something he had received from his Creator. His wisdom became corrupted, and he challenged the authority of God and led an open rebellion against the great Creator. He wanted His "more excellent name." He wanted to be God. He wanted God's place and God's power and God's praise.

Satan suffered from an "I" problem. In Isaiah 14:13-14 the five "I wills" of Satan are recorded:
"I will ascend into heaven."
"I will exalt my throne above the stars of God."
"I will sit also upon the mount."
"I will ascend above the heights of the clouds."
"I will be like the most High."

The only thing left for our Heavenly Father to do was to cast Lucifer out of His presence, take him from his responsible position, and put him under a curse. The Book of Revelation tells us about the great war in heaven that resulted. Satan was overpowered, and he and all of his rebellious angels were cast out of heaven.

From that day to this, Satan as a fallen creature has hated God with fierce vengeance, and he is bent on one purpose, that is, to set aside the Son of God and steal all the worship from men and angels alike. This is the great controversy that is now being carried out on the planet earth.

Because Satan tried to exalt himself above God he was thrown down, cast out, dethroned. He lost his exalted position and an angel of God became the devil. Lucifer in his fall became Satan.

Like a Roaring Lion

What is Satan like? Peter said Satan is like a roaring lion who walks about seeking whom he may devour (1 Pet. 5:8). This verse does not describe Satan's appearance but his character. The devil does not look like a lion; he acts like one. He is ferocious in nature, vicious in character, and relentless in his pursuit.

The image that lies behind what Peter said is that of a shepherd watching over his flock by night. Often during the night a lion would stalk and circle the flock, seeking which sheep he could devour. That's the way our adversary is.

First Peter 5:8 is not the first time in Scripture that Satan is pictured as a wild, ferocious beast. In Genesis 4:1-7, a contention arose between Cain and Abel over their worship of God. Abel's sacrifice was accepted, but Cain's was rejected. Jealousy, anger, and resentment welled up in Cain. The Lord spoke a warning to him, "If thou doest well, shalt thou not be accepted? and if thou doest not well, sin lieth at the door" (v. 7). This is the first time the word *sin* appears in the Bible. It is described as lying at the door. The word *lie* means to crouch on all four legs like an animal. Sin is personified as a wild animal lurking in a charging position.

Satan does not appear as a roaring lion. I wish he did; he would be easier to resist. He appeared to Eve as a shining serpent, offering her a better life (Gen 3:1). He appeared to Jesus as a concerned friend, trying to prevent Him from going to the cross (Matt. 16:23). He appeared to the Corinthians as an angel of light, preaching the truth of God (2 Cor. 11:14). And he does the same with us. He cleverly disguises himself as one who will do us good, but in reality he is out to do us in.

In the world of international espionage, governments sometimes employ beautiful, alluring women who are paid to seduce high-ranking government officials. The women's assignments are to discover some of the enemy's military secrets. That is how Satan works. He is not only beautiful and seductive but also treacherous. When expedient, Satan can be a perfect gentleman. Stylishly dressed, he may approach us with the proposition: "Sell me your soul and I'll make you rich and happy."

He appears to us as "the man of distinction" with a cocktail in one hand and a cigarette in the other. But he is not the man of distinction. He is the man of *extinction*. With both of these tools, the cocktail and the cigarette, he will destroy us if he can.

He will appear to us as a brilliant and gifted preacher or teacher, speaking in learned eloquence. But he denies the faith. He empties the Scriptures of their inspiration. He takes away deity from Christ and makes Him just another man. He robs the church of its hope of a glorious tomorrow. That is Satan.

He appears as a great and popular leader of government who comes forth as a champion of the people. He soothes us into believing that he is our great benefactor and patron. He is smart, shrewd, and deceptive, but beyond his soft voice is destruction and ruin. He is out to devour, consume, gulp us down.

Satan's first goal is to keep us from becoming Christians. If he fails there, his goal is to render us ineffective as Christians. He does not want us to be happy, confident, or useful in our faith. If he can rob us of our assurance, our joy, and our usefulness, he has rendered us ineffective and nullified our testimony.

Why Doesn't God Kill the Devil?

You may be wondering, as people have wondered through the years, why God doesn't kill the devil? Why does He allow him to go on?

We cannot understand evil in the world or in the human heart. In Revelation 10:7 the apostle John, by inspiration, wrote that when the seventh angel sounds the mystery of God will be finished. Why God allows Satan and evil and darkness in His universe is unknown to us. Why does not the Lord, by the sweep of the hand, or by the word of His voice, destroy all evil? Why, we do not know. It is called in the Scriptures "the musterion"—the secret of evil which is not revealed to us.

We can only guess. When God created the angelic realm, He didn't want robots. He wanted creatures who could respond to His love and have spontaneous fellowship with Him. He took a calculated risk by giving them self-determination, but He believed it was worth the risk, so He created these beings with the ability to act independently of Him.

God's purpose seems to be to make a sufficient and final trial of every claim of His adversaries. He allows Satan to exist because He wants us to see what happens when evil runs its full and final course. Thus, when this age with its developments shall have passed by, every mouth will be stopped, and the whole world and Satan will know their own failure and sin before God. The patience of God infinitely transcends our own.

Another probable reason for the delay in the termination of evil in the world is that the presence of evil provides the Christian with a ceaseless conflict, through which one can gain the character of an overcomer. This character in the sight of God is vital and priceless. It also provides the Christian the privilege of being a witness. By faithful testimony against the enemy of God, the believer is able to gain one's crown and reward.

Though no one has the final answer, we can see these as a part of God's purpose.

Victory in Jesus

How can we be victorious over our adversary? What is our hope? We must "resist stedfast in the faith" (1 Pet. 5:9). The word *resist* is a military term that means to stand against another's onset. We cannot fight the devil. He was originally a powerful and wise angel God created. He still retains much of this wisdom and power, as a glance down the pages of history and a look about today will show. But while we cannot take the offensive, we can stand our ground in the face of Satan's attacks. The devil is like any bully; he retreats when he is gallantly and bravely resisted in the strength and the company of Jesus Christ. That is what we must do.

We are to "resist stedfast." The word *steadfast* is a term used of material objects to denote solidarity. No superficial faith will do against Satan. Winston Churchill once said of General Tutor, "The impression I had of Tutor was an iron peg hammered into frozen ground—immovable." That's the way we are to be toward Satan.

And, we are to "resist steadfast in the faith." No resistance will be successful in our own strength. Our faith and trust in Christ must be like a solid wall against which the devil attacks in vain.

This is an aggressive, not a passive warfare. It is not enough for us to assume that because we have Christ as our Savior and are on the victor's side we can afford to ignore Satan. Truly he is not able to devour all whom he hates, but he can trip us up and cause our ministry for the

Lord to be hindered. We are to resist him steadfast in the faith, which calls for a close walk with the Lord and, by faith, a constant close adherence to His Word.

Jesus' death on the cross has assured us of the full and final defeat of Satan. There the bruising of Satan's head, which was a part of the Adamic covenant, was realized. Referring to the cross, Jesus said, "Now is the judgment of this world: now shall the prince of this world be cast out" (John 12:31).

Someone told a reformed alcoholic: "I see you have mastered the devil at last." "No," came the quiet answer, "but I do have the Master of the devil." That is our hope also.

Though Satan's sentence has been passed, it has not yet been executed. That will happen at the end of the age. Until then he is "like a roaring lion," and every believer must contend with him. If we stand strong in the faith, we can win. Others have, and so can we.

2

Born-Again Christians with Birth Defects

We face an everday paradox. Many Christians call themselves "born-again Christians." Yet, they live inconsistently and put their Lord to an open shame. They act and speak out of character with their profession of faith. Indeed, they may well be born again, but they are "born-again believers with birth defects."

Some people think that once we become Christians we no longer have to struggle against temptation and sin. The fact is, once we become Christians, we can expect temptation not only to continue but also to intensify. As Christians, we are God's children. That makes us special to Him. And the more we mean to God, the more we mean to the devil. And the more effective we are in God's service, the more desperate will become the devil's attack on us.

When we become Christians, several wonderful things happen. Our sins are forgiven. We are adopted into the family of God. And we receive a new nature as a result of the Holy Spirit's coming to live in us. However, our old sin nature (called the flesh) is still in us also and remains unchanged. These two natures are contrary to and in constant conflict with one another (Gal. 5:17).

The Greek word translated *contrary* literally means "hostile." It is a military term that suggests a fierce and unrelenting civil war going on inside us to establish dominion over us. Old sinful impulses and carnal desires must be overcome if we are going to win in the Christian warfare. The truth is that in the spiritual conflict we have an adversary from without, called the devil, who has an ally within, called the flesh. Satan is not only the accuser but also the tempter who seeks to draw us away from God and into sin by appealing to our inner desires.

Satan's Bridgehead

The flesh, our old sinful nature, is the bridgehead through which sin enters our lives. Satan appeals to these inner desires or lusts and lures us away from God into sin. James used a vivid illustration on how Satan does this: "But each one is tempted when he is carried away and enticed by his own lust. But when lust has conceived, it brings forth sin; and when sin is accomplished, it brings forth death" (Jas. 1:14, 15 NASB).

The word *entice* is a fishing term. A fisherman doesn't drop a bare hook into the water. He baits the hook to interest and entice a fish. Sometimes the bait is a colorful, plastic worm. Sometimes it is a live wiggling minnow. Sometimes it is a tasty shrimp. He drops the bait into the water and keep it dancing, jiggling up and down to attract the attention of the fish. The fisherman hopes the fish will pass nearby and will be unable to resist the bait and will be hooked before he knows it.

Temptation always follows that same overall process. Notice how it works:

Step 1: The bait is dropped.
Step 2: The inner desire is attracted to the bait.
Step 3: We bite the bait; we yield to the temptation and sin.

Step 4: We end up hooked and cooked. That's the tragic consequence of sin.

Satan appeals to our inner desires. Without that he would have little chance of leading us into sin.

The thrust of temptation is always the same: The one who is below us (Satan) appeals to that which is within us (our desire) to draw us from the one who is above us (God).

If a spark falls on water, nothing happens. If a spark falls on ice, nothing happens. If a spark falls on glass or marble, nothing happens. But if a spark falls on a powder keg, there is a tremendous explosion. Our desires, our lusts, are like a powder keg ready to explode at almost any moment.

As a result of this inner conflict between the flesh and the spirit, we shouldn't be surprised if we act in ways we never thought we would. We find ourselves doing things that we don't want to do and not doing things that we want to do (Gal. 5:17; Rom. 7:19).

Let me illustrate. I have a friend who became a Christian several years ago. He grew up without benefit of a Christian home. In high school he was a good amateur boxer. Later he became a policeman and eventually was an undercover narcotics agent. Fighting and violence were a part of his early life.

After his conversion he became dedicated to Christ. He won many of his old friends to Christ, began teaching a Sunday School class, and was ordained a deacon. One night he and a friend were participating in church visitation. After they had made their visits, they stopped by a restaurant for a cup of coffee. A man sitting at the counter of the restaurant started making some derogatory remarks about our denomination. Our city was in a liquor election at the time, and the man said in a loud voice, "Those ____ ____ Baptists! If it weren't for them, we could have liquor in Tyler." On and on he went.

Finally my friend had all he could take. He rolled up his Bible, walked up to the man, and said, "Mister, I'm a Baptist, and if you say one more word about my church I am going to cram this Bible down your throat."

Can you imagine that: Out visiting for Christ one moment and threatening to whip a man the next? How can you explain that? It is easy. My friend's old nature asserted itself at that moment and made him angry and violent. Those are characteristics of our old nature.

If the story had ended there, we might wonder about my friend's dedication. However, the next morning he came to my house greatly distressed. He had been planning to go as a lay preacher with me on a mission trip to the West Indies. Now he was wondering if he should back out. After telling me what had happened the night before, he said, "How can a man who acts like I did go and preach to others?"

We talked awhile, and I explained to him about the two natures that were struggling within him. When he understood what had happened, he seemed relieved. Every night for the next week he went back to that cafe hoping to see that man again so he could apologize to him for his actions.

That was a remarkable change in my friend. Before he became a Christian, he would have been proud of what he said to that man. Now he was ashamed of it. Before, he would have bragged about it. Now he was apologizing for it. His old nature had made him angry. His new nature had made him ashamed. His flesh had made him want to fight. The Spirit had made him want to apologize. Every Christian knows something about that kind of struggle.

Understanding Temptation

As long as we live, we will have struggles with our flesh. There will never be a time, this side of heaven, when we are free from it. All people, no matter how spiritual they are, are susceptible to temptation. We never conquer Satan; we only withstand him.

Several facts about temptation will aid our understanding. First, to be tempted is not a sin. Jesus was tempted at all points, just as we are, yet He was without sin (Heb. 4:15). Sin occurs only when we yield to temptation. Billy Sunday put it this way: "Temptation is Satan knocking at the door. Sin is opening the door and inviting him in."

Second, we do not have to sin when we are tempted. People today want a scapegoat to deliver them from personal responsibility for their sins. But none exists. Nothing outside ourselves is strong enough—not even Satan—to cause us to sin. Satan is not coequal with God. He is a created being who can tempt but not force.

Sin takes place when we agree to the temptation and follow it. It takes agreement on our part. Not until I individually involve myself does sin take place.

The assurance we have from the Lord that we do not have to sin is His promise that He will never allow us to be tempted beyond our power to resist (1 Cor. 10:13).

Some bridges have signs on them that state their load limit. That is the amount of weight that the highway engineers have determined the bridge can safely bear without collapsing. In the same way God, the Master Engineer who created us from conception, knows how much strain we can endure without collapsing under the weight of temptation. And He limits the tempting power of Satan in our lives. Satan can act only within the limits set by divine sovereignty.

Third, Christ understands what we are going through when we are tempted and will help us to withstand it. The writer of Hebrews encouraged steadfastness in Christian faith when he wrote, "We have not a high priest which cannot be touched with the feeling of our infirmities; but was in all points tempted like as we are, yet without sin. Let us therefore come boldly unto the throne of grace, that we may obtain mercy, and find grace to help in time of need" (Heb. 4:15-16). The Greek word translated *help* means "to strengthen." It refers to a rope or a chain frapping a vessel. It is the same word used in Acts 27:17 to describe the undergirding of a ship.

While Paul was on his way to Rome, the ship he was traveling on was caught in a fierce storm and was about to be broken up by the winds and waves. As a last resort, the sailors wrapped huge chains around the hull of the ship to help hold it together. In the same way those sailors strengthened their ship to keep it from cracking up, so Christ strengthens us to withstand the storms of temptation. Without His help, His support, we too would crack up. A part of the good news of the gospel is that supporting chains in the form of divine grace are available to us.

But where can we get this help? How can we have God's grace in our lives? We find grace to help through prayer. Hebrews 4:16 invites us to come to "the throne of grace." The throne of grace is the place of prayer. Prayer is always the gateway to getting help from God.

Second, we get grace to help through Bible study. Peter wrote, "Grace and peace be multiplied unto you through the knowledge of God, and of Jesus our Lord" (2 Pet. 1:2). Spiritual mathematics are fascinating. By adding to our Bible knowledge we multiply grace in our lives.

When dealing with the devil: Don't argue, quote. That's what Jesus did. He met every satanic temptation with a

Scripture quotation. In Jesus' first recorded encounter with Satan, when He was tempted to turn stones into bread, Jesus said, "It is written, Man shall not live by bread alone, but by every word that proceedeth out of the mouth of God" (Matt. 4: 4; see Deut. 8:3).

When Satan suggested that Jesus cast Himself from the pinnacle of the Temple, He responded, "It is written again, Thou shalt not tempt the Lord by God" (v. 7, see Deut. 6:16).

When Satan promised to give Jesus all the kingdoms of the world if He would but bow down and worship him, Jesus responded, "It is written, Thou shalt worship the Lord thy God, and him only shalt thou serve" (v. 10; see Deut. 6:13).

Notice the recurring phrase Jesus used: "It is written . . ." The Word of God memorized and stored up within us becomes for us, as it was for Christ, an inner brace against the outer pressures of temptation.

The final way to get grace is through humility. Peter wrote, "God resisteth the proud, and giveth grace to the humble" (1 Pet. 5:5). God never gives His strengthening grace to the proud. It is reserved for those who sincerely trust in Him.

If we are going through moral or marital or emotional storms, we need to check our spiritual chains. We may have no undergirding from God because we have neglected prayer, Bible study, and a humble spirit. Without these we're all sunk.

Stand! Walk! Run!

How can we win this fierce and unrelenting battle against the flesh and the devil? We can stand, we can walk, and we can run.

The Scriptures say, "Resist the devil, and he will flee

from you" (Jas. 4:7). The Greek word *resist* is another military word. It means "to take your stand against, to withstand" the embattled forces of evil. Some people have made resisting temptation some mystical, unreachable, unattainable virtue reserved for the very pious. Fiddlesticks! Saying no is something all of us who belong to Christ can do. There is nothing magical about it. We simply put Jesus Christ at the helms of our lives and say no!

If you keep on resisting the devil he will flee from you. Think of that! Resist the devil again and again every time an evil thought or doubt comes back. Refuse to give up your position. And, sooner or later, inevitably, the doubts will clear, your feelings will change, the attacks cease, and you will be back in the sunshine of faith and the experience of the love and joy of God.

Second, we can walk! "Walk in the Spirit, and ye shall not fulfill the lust of the flesh" (Gal. 5:16). The verb Paul used more than thirty times is in the present tense here and speaks of habitual action: "keep on walking." To walk in the Spirit is to live a life of continuous dependence upon the Lord. In myself I lack the power to overcome Satan. I can't do it. You can't do it. But He can! He is in us (1 John 4:4).

Third, we can run! Paul wrote, "But put ye on the Lord Jesus Christ, and make not provision for the flesh, to fulfil the lust thereof" (Rom. 13:14). The word *provision* suggests the idea of forethought. Some people dream of sin, imagine sin, and, if granted the opportunity, indulge in sin. Don't overmatch yourself with Satan. Don't give the flesh an opportunity to assert itself by putting yourself in a compromising situation. There is a time to fight and there is a time for flight.

Joseph is a classic example of how to handle temptation in this way. Joseph worked for an important Egyptian government official. The duties of office often carried Potiphar away from home. While he attended to state affairs, his wife envisioned affairs of her own. She became attracted to Joseph. He was young, handsome, and single —and always around. So the lovely, lonely Mrs. Potiphar asked Joseph to go to bed with her.

Joseph was a normal male with normal hormones. So her invitation must have been a real temptation to him. But Joseph refused her, saying, "Behold, with me here, my master does not concern himself with anything in the house, and he has put all that he owns in my charge. There is no one greater in this house than I, and he has withheld nothing from me except you, because you are his wife. How then could I do this great evil, and sin against God?" (Gen. 39:8-9, NASB).

Isn't that great! Joseph answered with a resounding no. But the captain's wife came back again. The next time she caught his garment, saying, "Lie with me!" he left his garment in her hand and fled and went outside (Gen. 39:10-12).

Joseph took off to let her cool off. He ran like mad. That's what it means to "give no occasion to the flesh." Learn from Joseph, run!

Don't play the fool by constantly flirting with temptation. You are playing right into the hand of the devil. Don't think that once you have resisted temptation it will end. Satan doesn't give up easily.

Life without temptations would be wonderful. But fleshly desires will always rage within us, and Satan will constantly appeal to them. Our only hope is to resist them in the faith, walk in the spirit, and abstain from the very appearance of evil.

That's the way to win in the spiritual warfare.

3

The God of This World

Following the Battle of Egypt, in the early days of World War II, Winston Churchill made one of his famous speeches. He said, "Now this is not the end. It is not even the beginning of the end. But it is, perhaps, the end of the beginning."

What was true of the Battle of Egypt is also true of the Christian warfare. Conversion is not the end of the Christian struggle; it is not even the beginning of the end; it is just the end of the beginning. A lifetime of spiritual conflict will follow.

We fight the Christian battle on three fronts! These are commonly referred to as the world, the flesh, and the devil. We have an enemy without—the devil. He has an ally within us—the flesh. And we contend against him in a hostile atmosphere—the world.

Satan is called in Scripture "the god of this world" (2 Cor. 4:4) What that means, in part, is that he always has the homefield advantage against us; we are always playing in his ball park. Militarily it means we fight him in hostile territory. He has the populace, the masses, on his side against us.

The Greek word translated *world* is the word *aion* which means age. It is used here in a moral and spiritual sense. It refers to the spirit of this age as opposed to the age to come. Worldliness is a mental attitude that excludes God from life. It encompasses everything in the existing order of things which is outside the kingdom of God.

Each of us has a certain life-style. Behind that life-style is a value system or a philosophy of life. Our value system or philosophy of life determines our dress, our morals, and our behavior. There are only two sources for our value system: the world or the Word.

According to the Bible, the whole social structure of this world is controlled by a prevailing principle of life that is foreign to God and leads people away from Him. Through education, music, art, styles, the mass media, and government, the god of this world exerts tremendous pressure on all of us to conform to the world's life-style rather than God's. That is why Paul wrote, "Don't let the world around you squeeze you into its own mould" (Rom. 12:2, Phillips). This subtle pressure is another way Satan gets to us. He uses the pull of the flesh from within and the pressure of the world from without. If we aren't careful, we will unwittingly permit ourselves to be influenced more by what people say than by what God says. This can happen gradually, almost imperceptibly, but it can happen, nonetheless.

This subtle change reminds me of the story I heard once about a rather hideous experiment in which some frogs were placed in a bowl of water. The water was heated very gently; by the time it was boiling, all the frogs were dead. None of them made any attempt to get out because the heating was done so gradually. I would suggest that the church today is like those frogs. We have allowed the pressures and the pleasures of the world to entice and entrap us until, in many ways, our lives are not discernably different from those of our unbelieving neighbors.

How does Satan exert influence over our age? How does he rule the world? As a bogus god he gets some people to worship him. Satan worship is real. But that is not his chief tactic. He is far too subtle for that. Most often he blinds or obscures people's minds to the truth of God and causes them to believe lies. Don't expect honesty or fair play from him.

Satan is a liar, the father of lies (John 8:44). In his classic allegory, *The Holy War,* John Bunyan presented Satan's tactics. Although the great fortress, Mansoul, is beseiged by enemy forces, they can enter only if the gates are opened from the inside. Diabolus's strategy to persuade the defenders to open their gates to him is to "delude them, pretending things that will never be and promising things they shall never get. Lies, lies, lies . . . ."

Satan is the master of deceit, especially at the use of illusions. Samuel Baker told of a regiment dying of thirst in the Nubian Desert. The soldiers thought they saw water in the distance, but their Arabian guide warned that it was only a mirage. They argued, the guide was killed, and the whole regiment rushed toward the water. Mile after mile the mirage led the thirsty troops deeper into the desert. Too late they realized the truth. They died pursuing a fantasy.

That's the way Satan does. Using soap operas, movies, and erotic literature, as well as other means, he leads us away from God. He causes millions to base powerful fantasies on the lie that man's way is better than God's way.

John graphically described the three most common lies Satan deposits in human minds when he wrote:

> Love not the world, neither the things that are in the world. If any man love the world, the love of the Father is not in him. For all that is in the world, the lust of the

flesh, and the lust of the eyes, and the pride of life, is not of the Father, but is of the world. And the world passeth away, and the lusts thereof: but he that doeth the will of God abideth forever (1 John 2:15-17).

In these verses are found the three dominant thought systems or philosophies of our present age. They are:

Hedonism—The belief that pleasure is the chief end of life

Materialism—The belief that things are the chief value of life

Humanism—The belief that man is the chief actor of life

But these are only illusions of Satan. He uses them to blind our minds to the truth of the gospel. He leads us to believe that life and pleasure are found in gratifying our sensual cravings in what money can buy, in what the eyes can see, and in arrogant independence of God. He has done a brainwashing job on the earth. Worldiness is a life in which there is no future. As usual, Satan promises more than he can produce.

Grab for the Gusto

The first great lie that Satan uses to deceive us is hedonism. The motto of the hedonist is, "If it feels good, do it." His theme song is, "You only go around once in life, so grab for all the gusto you can get."

This belief isn't new or modern. It is as old as Eden. It was hedonism when Eve saw that the forbidden fruit was good for food, pleasant to the eyes, and desired to make one wise, and she ate (Gen. 3:6). The motto of the Epicureans of ancient Greece was, "Let us eat, drink and be merry for tomorrow we die." Paul spoke of some people in his day, as "enemies of the cross of Christ: . . . whose

God is their belly, and whose glory is in their shame" (Phil. 3:18-19). Their god was their appetite, and they boasted of things that they should have blushed about. Paul warned Timothy that the time would come when men would be lovers of pleasures more than lovers of God (2 Tim. 3:4). These are all expressions of hedonism.

A careful study of God's Word reveals three specific kinds of pleasure—sinful pleasure, legitimate pleasure, and eternal pleasure.

For forty years Moses indulged in the wisdom and wealth of Egypt. All of the opportunities of that great nation were his, but he turned his back on it all, "choosing rather to suffer affliction with the people of God, than to enjoy the pleasures of sin for a season" (Heb. 11:25). Let's be honest. Sinful pleasure provides enjoyment. Satan is not such a fool as to fish without bait.

All pleasures, of course, are not sinful. God intends for His children to enjoy many legitimate pleasures. Paul wrote to Timothy that "the living God . . . giveth us richly all things to enjoy" (1 Tim. 6:17). Each of us should make time for legitimate pleasure. A bow kept under constant tension loses its resilience. So it is with us. If we don't relax occasionally, we will be basket cases or casket cases.

But we must be on guard. If Satan can't get us through sinful pleasures, he'll get us through seemingly legitimate ones. Supposedly innocent pleasures can choke the spiritual strength out of our lives. Sometimes so simple a thing as a boat or a lake house develops into an idol. An innocent hobby can become an obsession.

While this world offers some temporary pleasure, God's Word talks about another kind of pleasure. David said, "Thou wilt show me the path of life: in thy presence is fulness of joy; at thy right hand, there are pleasures for evermore" (Ps. 16:11). This is eternal pleasure, lasting pleasure, pleasure forevermore.

The world by and large is always brainwashing us to believe that pleasure is the chief end of life. Satan will, if he can, catch us in a flesh trap. Even if he doesn't get us, we live in a world in which hedonism is believed, in which we must contend against Satan. It simply makes a hard fight even more difficult. We must firmly reject the lie of this world that pleasure is the chief end of life. It is not. God is.

Don't Choke to Death

A second great lie of Satan is materialism. It is the belief that things are the chief value of life—cars, boats, houses, clothes, and the like.

In ancient days people believed that the world ended just beyond the Straits of Gibraltar. Roman soldiers often roamed and camped deep inside the many tunnels there. Because they thought that a few miles further to the west lay the jumping-off place, they chiseled the words, *NE PLUS ULTRA:* "Nothing more beyond" in many places on the tunnel walls.

Many people look at this world with that same thought in mind; to them there is nothing more beyond this life. Paul described the enemies of the cross of Christ as those "who mind earthly things" (Phil. 3:19). He meant by that phrase that the earth was the limit to their horizons. They saw nothing beyond it.

Jesus gave us the classic compelling story of an out-and-out materialist. A successful farmer worked hard, lived frugally, and planned carefully until he had everything he needed in life. The man became so intent on accumulating material goods that he forgot all other values. He tore down his old barns to build even larger ones and said to himself, "Soul, thou hast much goods laid up for many years; take thine ease, eat, drink, and be merry." The climax comes as God says to him, "Thou fool" (Luke 12:16-20). The man died, leaving everything behind.

The man made three terribly foolish mistakes. First, he mistook his soul for his body. Second, he mistook himself for God. Finally, he mistook time for eternity.

Jesus did not consider working to accumulate goods to be wrong; rather, He consistently emphasized the necessity of giving priority to the spiritual in our lives. Haven't you lived long enough to observe that just about the time a man says, "I've got it made," time runs out on him?

Jesus told the story of another farmer who planted a field of grain. Some of the seed fell on hard ground and were eaten by the birds. Some seed fell on shallow ground, and the plants soon withered because the soil was not deep. Some of the seed fell among the thorns, and the tender plants were soon choked out by them. And some of the seed fell on good soil and reproduced abundantly.

Jesus didn't tell this parable to teach us a lesson in agriculture; He told it to teach us about life. The seed in the parable represent the gospel. The thorns represent "the cares of this world, and the deceitfulness of riches" (Mark 4:19).

This is one of Jesus' most solemn warnings in life. Things can easily choke the gospel out of our lives. We can get so caught up in the pursuit of things that our love for God and dedication to those things spiritual gradually ebb away.

Right at this moment some of us have fallen prey to materialism. We are overcommitted to our businesses and are undercommitted to the Lord. Our careers, our professions, our businesses are far more important to us than spiritual things. Nothing pleases Satan more.

None of us, not even Christian workers, is ever safe from the corrosive effects of both money and power. Paul warned Timothy, "No man that warreth entangleth himself with the affairs of this life; that he may please him who hath chosen him to be a soldier" (2 Tim. 2:4).

And while I do not wish to take an extreme position that equates poverty with spirituality, I think many Christians need to take a hard second look at what the Gospels have to say about the use and abuse of wealth. Jesus dealt with this very succinctly. He never said that material success was wrong. He simply stated a fact about human nature which we seem to have forgotten: where our treasure is, there will our heart be also. We cannot serve two masters; we cannot serve God and material possessions simultaneously.

The late Grady Nutt, a long time friend of mine who used to be a regular on the television program "Hee Haw," told of attending a small Christian college years ago. He said that it was located five miles from any known sin. "The school has three rules," said Grady. "You won't smoke, you won't drink, and you won't want to." He said, "I was dismissed for wanting to."

Well, wanting to is where sin begins. The titanic truth of Scripture is that all good and bad begins in our heads. Our lives will be successful in direct proportion to that which we desire.

Watch your desires! Don't let your passion for possessions get your life out of perspective. Remember the Commandment of our Lord, "Thou shalt not covet . . ." (Ex. 20:17). Covetousness begins in the mind. It is first a thought then an act. Remember the caution of Paul, "The love of money is the root of all evil" (1 Tim. 6:10).

A time comes when each follower of Christ must ask, How do I feel about things? If I love Christ, how do I feel about my possessions? How do I treat my money? How in heaven's name do I treat earth's things?

Four Rotten Pillars

The third lie of Satan is humanism. Humanism is the belief that man is the chief actor of life. It makes man the center and the circumference of all of life. It eliminates God from life and makes man God.

Man, of course, is the crown of God's creation. The Bible tells us that in the beginning God took a lump of clay and shaped man's physical features. But at that point man was nothing more than a statue. Then God breathed into man the breath of life and he became a living soul.

All creatures have life, but only man has the life of God in him—intelligence, moral capacity, and will. Man can do many things. He can build a spaceship that will sail to the moon and back. He can build a satellite that will broadcast messages instantaneously around the world. He can build a submarine that will sail around the earth under water. But man is still a creature. He is not God.

Humanism is built on four rotten pillars: The first is atheism: There is no God. The second is evolution: Man evolved from lower forms of life. He was not created. The third is amorality: There are no moral absolutes in life. The fourth is the deification of man: We are our own god.

If there is no God, man was not created; he evolved from some lower form of life to what he is today, the highest of the animals. If man is only an animal, he is neither moral nor immoral. As an animal he lives only for self-gratification, self-preservation, and self-propagation. There are no moral and ethical absolutes in life. Right is what he feels good after and wrong is what he feels bad after. Man is his own god. There is nothing or no one higher.

Many people believe humanism has infiltrated governments, education, media, and the arts.

What are the results of humanism? Some are sexual permissiveness, trial marriages, abortion on demand, easy divorce, inflammatory sex education, coed dormitories, homosexuality as an optional life-style, easy access to pornography, and a drug-oriented society. As result of the humanistic philosophy, America is reeling in drunkenness and rotting in promiscuity. Our entertainment has reached the limits of filth.

These lies—hedonism, materialism, and humanism—lure us until we are caught like a fly in a spider's web. People get caught up in a desire for pleasure, for possessions, and for prestige, and their love for God and devotion to those things spiritual ebb away. Prayer, Bible study, and church attendance are soon gone. Then it is only a matter of time until it can be said of them as it was said of Demas, "Demas hath forsaken me, having loved this present world" (2 Tim. 4:10). The world gets an awful stranglehold on the spiritual lives of people and drags them down to darkness and death. In this kind of atmosphere, we must live and contend with Satan.

Is there any hope for victory? Yes! The good news is, "Greater is he that is in you, than he that is in the world" (1 John 4:4). Satan is in the world and he is mighty. But Christ is in us and He is mightier still. Through His indwelling presence we can win the battle against the world, the flesh, and the devil. We can be more than conquerors. We can win in the spiritual warfare.

4

The Battle for the Mind

We never have it made in the Christian life. There is never a time when we can unbuckle our armor, lay down our sword, and take R. and R. No matter how close we may have walked with Jesus, no matter how clear our perception of the truth may have been, no matter how sincere a confession we may have made, we are always susceptible to backsliding, regressing to a lower spiritual level.

Peter the apostle is an example of this. Peter's experience at Caesarea Philippi is a classic case study in backsliding.

As Jesus and the apostles entered the region, He asked them two questions. The first was a leading question. He asked, "Whom do men say that I the Son of man am?" (John 16:13). This was not the question of an insecure leader seeking to know how he stood in the public opinion polls. It was a probing inquiry designed to determine the depths of their understanding as to who He was and why He had come.

The responses were quite complimentary. The disciples said that He was being called John the Baptist, Elijah, Jeremiah, or one of the prophets.

Jesus then asked a deeper question, "Whom say ye that I am?" (v. 15). This is life's ultimate question. Our answer to this question determines our relationship to God, our capacity for life, our character and conduct, how we face death, and our eternal destiny.

Peter responded, "Thou art the Christ, the Son of the living God" (v. 16). In that moment Peter realized who Jesus really was—the Messiah, the promised One of God. He was the Savior foretold by the prophets. This insight had come not by human reason but by divine revelation.

With this deeper understanding by the disciples, Jesus told them that He had to go to Jerusalem where death awaited Him. That was utterly unthinkable to Peter. He had sifted through prophecy and had concluded that the Messiah would establish an earthly kingdom, sit on the throne of David, and rule the world from Jerusalem. A crown he could accept. A cross was utterly incomprehensible.

Peter was strong-willed; once he made up his mind it was hard to change him. So he argued with Jesus. "God forbid it, Lord! This shall never happen to You" (v. 22, NASB).

What audacity! Peter the apostle rebuked the Lord of glory. He thought he knew more about God's business then God did. This kind of strong-mindedness makes one a good leader but a poor disciple. Simon's problem was that he was still controlled by Simon. He had not yielded the control room of his life to the Lord.

Jesus' response was shocking. He said, "Get thee behind me, Satan: for thou art an offence unto me: for thou savourest not the things that be of God, but those that be of men" (v. 23). Jesus heard in Simon's reply more than misguided love or spiritual confusion. He believed at that moment Peter had become a pawn, a mouthpiece of Satan to divert Him from God's will for His life.

Momentarily Satan had taken control of Peter's life and

uttered words for which he had to be rebuked by our Savior. For the time being, Satan had possessed Peter's mind and thoughts and had spoken through him. The Lord Jesus did not say, "Get thee behind me, Peter," but "Get thee behind me, Satan." Satan was speaking through Peter, so it is no wonder the utterances were at variance with the revealed will of God.

This experience suggests one of the most profound truths in the Bible. We can be on God's side one minute and on Satan's side the next. We can be the voice of revelation in one breath and the voice of temptation in the next. We can move from the great confession to the great collapse in five short verses.

Peter was the first man to confess, "Thou art the Christ." But he also became a tool of Satan to divert Jesus from God's will. If it could happen to Simon Peter, it can happen to us. The proximity of these two statements— "Thou art the Christ" and "Get thee behind me, Satan"— point up the danger of backsliding.

Satan's first effort is always to keep us from becoming Christians. If he fails in that, his second effort is to cause us to backslide to a lower spiritual state so that he can use us for his purposes.

Three pertinent truths concerning backsliding are in this experience. (1) Satan would like to make us an extension of evil in the world. (2) The battlefield for our lives is our minds. (3) We are never more vulnerable than immediately following our greatest spiritual experience. Surely these are the reasons so many good Christians do so many bad things.

Extensions of Evil

Christians need to understand two great companion truths in the Bible. The first is that we, the church, are the body of Christ on earth. Once our Lord incarnated Himself for thirty-three years in a human body. In the days of His flesh, Jesus had eyes with which to see the hurt of His world, ears with which to hear its cry, feet to carry Him to its side, hands with which to minister to it, and lips with which to speak to it the word of God. After Christ ascended bodily into heaven, His living Spirit came to dwell in us. Today He perpetually incarnates Himself in His new body, the church. The Holy Spirit does not haunt houses. He dwells in people. Our bodies are the temple of His Spirit.

In the courtyard of a quaint little church in a French village stood a beautiful statue of Jesus with His hands outstretched. One day during World War II a bomb struck too close to the statue, and it shattered. After the battle was over, the citizens of the village decided to find pieces of their beloved statue and reconstruct it. Patiently they gathered the broken pieces and reassembled them. The scars on the body added to its beauty. But there was one problem. They were unable to find the hands of the statue. "A Christ without hands is no Christ at all," somebody lamented. "Hands with scars, yes. But what's a Lord without hands? We need a new statue." Someone else had another idea, and it prevailed. A brass plaque was attached to the base of the statue which read, "I have no hands but your hands."

We are the body of Christ on earth today. As such He intends for us to become an extension of Himself in the world. Through our bodies He ministers to the hurts and needs of people. God wants us to be His instruments to those around us.

The parallel truth is this: Just as we can become extensions of good, we can also become extensions of evil. This is evidenced by the fact that Jesus said to Peter, "Get thee behind me, Satan: for thou art an offence unto me."

The word *offense* means a hindrance or a stumbling block. At that moment Peter became the incarnation of Satan. He heard in Peter's words the same temptation He had struggled with in the wilderness. Following His baptism, Jesus was led by the Spirit into a wilderness region where He was tempted by the devil (Luke 4:1-12). Jesus was led to a place of solitude to decide on His messianic methods, and Satan came along to divert Him from doing God's will. Anytime the Spirit of God leads us anywhere, we can be sure Satan will be nearby. He is always close at hand to attempt to lead us from God's plan for our lives. In that experience Satan tempted Jesus at three points. First, he encouraged Jesus to turn stone into bread and satisfy His physical hunger (vv. 3-4). Then he offered Jesus the power and glory of world dictatorship if He would worship him. Finally, he suggested that Jesus test God by leaping from a high place on the Temple.

Satan even quoted a scriptural promise from God to support his suggestion. However, he quoted it out of context and applied it contrary to its initial meaning. He is never above that.

The wilderness temptations were aimed at one purpose —to divert Jesus from the will of God. God's will was that Jesus redeem the world through the cross. That required self-denial. Satan tempted Jesus to use His power for self-gratification instead. God's will was that Christ establish a spiritual kingdom. Satan tempted Jesus to establish an earthly, political kingdom. God's will for Christ was that He trust the Father completely. Satan tempted Jesus to He test God by taking an unnecessary risk.

At Caesara Philippi Peter was used by Satan to tempt Jesus in the same way He had been tempted in the wilderness. There was tremendous potential in Peter for both good and evil, for being either an instrument of God or an instrument of Satan.

The same is true of every one of us. We can become an extension of evil or of good in the world. What Satan did to and through Simon Peter he would also like to do to and through us.

If Satan cannot get to us through our desires, he will get to us through our friends. A misguided associate, an unbelieving mate, a hypocritical church member, a worldly parent—he will use anybody he can to thwart God's purpose. He will use them as extensions of his evil purposes to draw us away from the will of God. Nothing is quite as important as friends in our lives. Sometimes they are well meaning and unintentional in their influence toward evil, but it is strong, nonetheless. Satan delights in nothing more than to use people like you and me as an extension of evil in the world today. It is one of his primary tactics.

The World's Greatest Battlefield

The second truth about backsliding is that the mind is the battlefield where the spiritual conflict is waged. Jesus rebuked Peter, saying, "Thou savourest not the things that be of God, but those that be of men" (Matt. 16:23). The word "savourest" refers to the mind or cognitive faculties. It literally means "to regard" or "to think the same thing as."

Peter's problem was wrong thinking—humanistic thinking. He was thinking safety and security, while Jesus was thinking sacrifice and salvation. He was thinking of self, while Jesus was thinking of others. He was thinking crown, while Jesus was thinking cross. By rejecting the concept of the cross Peter became an easy prey to Satan.

The great battles of the world are not fought with guns

and bombs or by combat soldiers on the battlefields of this world; they are fought in the minds of people. The mind is the oldest, most common battlefield known to the human race. Ever since God provided Adam and Eve clear instructions on how to live happy, successful lives, a fierce battle has been raging over who will control man's thought processes—Satan or God.

In 2 Corinthians 10:3-5, Paul wrote, "Though we walk in the flesh, we do not war after the flesh: (For the weapons of our warfare are not carnal, but mighty through God to the pulling down of strong holds, Casting down imaginations and every high thing that exalteth itself against the knowledge of God, and bringing into captivity every thought to the obedience of Christ."

We are told three facts in these verses:
1. There is a battle.
2. The battle is fought in the mind.
3. The objective is to capture our thoughts.

The mind of man is here compared to an enemy's stronghold or fortress. Many evil thoughts, negative thoughts, are housed in this fortress and need to be taken captive to the obedience of Christ. These strong mental attitudes rise like a battalion of enemy soldiers in our minds. Paul recognized that we have to live in the world with its trouble and "in the flesh" with its frailties. But the real battle is spiritual. Satan's stronghold is our minds. He is ever seeking to capture our thoughts.

But God has not left us to the whims of the flesh or to Satan. We have been given the weapons we need to take "every thought captive to the obedience of Christ" (2 Cor. 10:5 NASB). Obedience is possible because of what Christ has already done. Because the victory was won on the cross, we have the right to evict thoughts that come from the flesh and the devil.

For us to be free from sinful thoughts, God Himself must be first in our thinking. Fellowship with God is the best deterrent for wrong and impure thoughts. We must fill our minds with truth, not vain imaginations. Soap operas, movies, and erotic literature have caused millions to base powerful fantasies on the lie that man's way is better than God's way. We must firmly reject these lies and meditate on the truth. Backsliding always begins in the mind, with wrong thinking. If the devil can get control of our minds, he has the control room of our lives.

Victories Are Dangerous

The third truth about backsliding is that we are most vulnerable to Satan following our greatest spiritual experiences. When is a championship team most likely to lose a game? Right after its biggest victory. Players become overconfident, they relax and let down, and suddenly they are upset. When is the Christian most likely to be defeated? Right after he has been on a spiritual high, he becomes an easy prey to Satan.

Many examples of this fact can be found in the Bible. After Samson single-handedly slew a thousand Philistines with a jawbone of a donkey, he laid his head in the lap of Delilah and was shorn of his power. When David was at the zenith of his political glory, he fell in love with another man's wife. Immediately following His baptism, after hearing the voice of God from heaven, Jesus was led into the wilderness where He was tempted of the devil. And, of course, Peter, intoxicated with the wine of his confession of Christ, became vulnerable to Satan's attack and immediately became his instrument. It can be the same with us.

The Bible warns, "Let him that thinketh he standeth take heed lest he fall" (1 Cor. 10:12). Pride always goes before destruction and a haughty spirit before a fall (Prov. 16:18).

The evil one is in the world today. He is doing battle in our minds in order to make us extensions of evil instead of good. And this is most likely to happen when we have just had our greatest spiritual experience with God.

The crucial issue in the spiritual warfare is our attitude toward the cross. If we can keep our thinking right about the cross, we can likely avoid backsliding. Humanistic thinking rejects the centrality of the cross, both for Jesus and for ourselves. However, Jesus makes it clear that we must accept both His cross and our own if we are going to be His disciples (Matt. 16:24).

Bess Arnold, a friend of mine, gave me a needlepoint picture for my study several years ago that depicts this truth. It reads, "No cross—No crown." It was so with Jesus; it is so with us.

We have even set this truth to music. We sing:

> Must Jesus bear the cross alone,
> And all the world go free?
> No there's a cross for everyone,
> And there's a cross for me.
> The consecrated cross I'll bear
> Till death shall set me free;
> And then go home my crown to wear,
> For there's a crown for me.

Commitment to Christ and the cross is the way to victory in the Christian warfare—and the way to avoid backsliding.

5

The Devil's Blockades

I had lunch with Forrest Feezor, former executive director of Texas Baptists, when he was ninety-one years old. Among the questions I asked him was what he would do differently if he had his life and his ministry to live over again. Dr. Feezor's answer surprised me. "Really not much," he said. "I have always sought to live by the will of God, and when you do that there is not much you would change."

Amen, Dr. Feezor. To find the will of God is life's greatest discovery. To do the will of God is life's greatest achievement. However, we should know from the outset that we will face tremendous obstacles. Satan will see to it. A part of his work is to hinder people from doing God's will.

The apostle Paul made this clear when he wrote, "Wherefore we would have come unto you, even I Paul, once and again; but Satan hindered us" (1 Thess. 2:18).

The Greek word translated "hindered" is *enkopto*. It literally means "to cut into" and was used of impeding persons by breaking up a road or by placing obstacles sharply in the path; hence, metaphorically it means to detain a person unnecessarily. It is a technical word for putting up a blockade calculated to stop an expedition on the march. In the days before TNT, tanks, and bazookas, the best way to stop a marching army was to burn a bridge or create an avalanche that would block the road. Paul said Satan did that to him.

Behind this verse is the fact that Paul had been separated from the Thessalonian Christians for quite some time, and he wrote to express his love for them and his anxiousness to see them. Then he gave a brief explanation for his extended absence from them after his forced departure. Lack of interest had not kept him from returning to them. Satan had hindered him.

Paul did not say how Satan hindered him. Perhaps the hindrance was the opposition of the Jews in Thessalonica. Perhaps it was an illness. Perhaps it was the pressure of other duties. We do not know. However, we do know that Satan always seeks to make impassable the roads of service for Christ. Paul had detected that subtle agency behind the difficulties he had in getting back to Thessalonica.

Paul used the word "hinder" in Galatians 5:7-8. "Ye did run well; who did hinder you that you should not obey the truth? This persuasion cometh not of him that calleth you." The Galatian Christians had been making splendid progress in the Christian race, but suddenly they went away from the truth. Paul asked them, "Who has interfered with you to hold you back from following the truth?" (TLB). Then he reminded them that certainly God had not held them back.

Hampering follow up and keeping believers from growing to maturity in Christ is at the heart of Satan's opposition to the body of Christ. If he could hinder an apostle in his follow up and if he could hinder early Christians in their Christian progress, is it any wonder we have problems?

These two passages teach us that Satan hinders us both

The Devil's Blockades

in the geographical (where God wants us to be) and in the operational (what God wants us to do) aspects of God's will.

Not just once, but again and again, Paul experienced hindrances from Satan. We don't have all the details of Satan's hindrances. All we know is that this verb reveals that Satan is in the business of putting blockades in the pathway of believers.

We cannot pursue the will of God without obstacles, difficulties, and opposition. Satan is opposed to God, and he will try to thwart our obedience to God's will. That is a part of Satan's work.

Do you feel a need for more prayer and Bible study? If so, resolve to find a place, set a time, and adopt a plan. Prayer and Bible study also take discipline. Satan will not allow such a resolve to go unhindered. He will raise blockades—a wandering mind, unusual pressure, or unexpected interruptions. Anticipate them, for they will come. Don't expect Satan to allow you to pursue this course unhindered. He delights in keeping us from daily family and private devotion. If he can win the battle against us there, he has won a major campaign in the spiritual warfare.

Do you feel a need for more regular attendance and worship? Most people do. If so, determine to become more faithful in church attendance. But don't think that this is an easy path to take. Satan will make it hard. How often I have heard people say, "I intended to be in church Sunday, but something came up." Sure it did. You know what it was? It was a blockade.

Do you feel a need for Christ in your life? Are you convicted of sin and are you convinced that Jesus is the Savior? If so, do you think Satan will allow you to come to Christ without obstacles? No! Not on your life.

Satan's greatest desire is to keep us from Christ. So, up goes a blockade. He will bring some inconsistent Christian across our pathway, attract our attention to a hypocrite, or plant the idea in our mind, *Wait until a more convenient season.* The road to hell is always paved with good intentions.

We should never expect to pursue God's will without such obstacles. We should anticipate them and recognize them for what they are. They are sure to come, and they come from Satan.

By now we have seen Satan as the accuser, the tempter, the deceiver, and the divider. Now we need to see him as the hinderer. I want to consider four of the most common blockades that Satan uses to hinder the people of God today.

Dealing with Doubts

The first, and perhaps most common, of Satan's blockades is doubt. He tries to get us to question the love and integrity of God. In the Garden God told Adam and Eve that they could eat of any of the trees except the tree of the knowledge of good and evil. He warned, "The day that thou eatest thereof thou shalt surely die" (Gen. 2:17).

When Satan appeared to Adam and Eve some time later, he asked, "Did God really say that?" When Eve said, "Yes," Satan replied, "Ye shall not surely die: For God doth know that in the day ye eat thereof, then your eyes shall be opened, and ye shall be as gods, knowing good and evil" (Gen. 3:4-5).

Satan's approach was to cause them to question the goodness and the honesty of God. According to Satan, God was not trying to protect them; He was trying to protect Himself. He did not want them to become gods.

The Devil's Blockades

If Satan can ever get us to doubt God, he can easily lead us away from God's will.

I have had to struggle with doubt all of my life. Faith has never come easy with me. Let me illustrate. Several years ago, I had some serious conflicts with a fellow Christian worker. I felt sure he not only had lied to me but he had lied about me repeatedly. The feelings between us were not good.

I was planning a trip to the city where he lived, and the Lord began to convict me that I needed to mend this broken relationship. The impression from God was very clear: I should seek him out and apologize for my part in our differences. Though I felt that he was the offender, I have lived long enough to know that no person is completely innocent in such conflicts. So, I prayed, "Lord, if you want me to talk to this man, make our paths to cross while I am visiting there this weekend." I had visited that city five or six times since I had moved away a few months earlier and our paths had never crossed, so I was asking for something unusual.

The first day I drove around the city quite a bit, visiting with old friends, but saw no trace of him. I thought of driving in front of his house. Perhaps he would be mowing the grass. But I decided that would be doing God's work for Him. So, I just kept praying about the matter.

The second day of my visit I picked up a friend and drove to a local cafe for a cup of coffee. As I took him home, I slowed down to pull into his driveway. Another car was approaching from the other direction, so I had to come to a complete stop for it to pass. Instead of driving on by, the on-coming car pulled up beside mine and stopped.

Who do you suppose it was? The very man I had been

praying about seeing! He rolled down his window and asked, "What are you doing?"

I replied, "Nothing, what are you doing?"

He said, "Let's go get a cup of coffee. We need to talk." So, he drove to the coffee shop, and I followed him. Would you believe that while I drove down the street behind him the thought came to my mind, *I wonder if God brought us together or is this just a coincidence?*"

That's the way I am. That's how skeptical I can be. I pray for something, it happens, and then I wonder if it was a coincidence. I tell you, faith comes hard for me. I am a skeptic by nature. It is not as a child that I believe.

I fight doubt with all of my might, and I nurse faith. I know the source of doubt. It and all negative thoughts come not from God but from Satan. It is one of the things he uses as a blockade to keep me from doing the will of God.

The Sting of Criticism

A second blockade of Satan is derision—the sneers, insults, innuendoes of our critics. Every faithful servant of God has had to face the biting criticism of others. The degenerates of Noah's day must have called him a fool for building an ark when it had never yet rained on the earth. Joseph's jealous brothers called him a dreamer (Gen. 37: 19). The congregation of Israel called Moses a dictator. "You take too much upon you," they said. (Num. 16:3). Elijah was called "[old] bald head" (2 Kings 2:23). Amos was called a hillbilly preacher from Tekoa. And Jesus was called everything under the sun. The apostle Paul, the greatest of all missionaries, was laughed to scorn in Athens and called a charlatan, a coward, an egotist, and a man pleaser by people in Corinth.

When do you suppose that the forces of evil were most

active on the earth? It was during the life and ministry of Jesus. Satan and his demons were more intense, more ferocious during that thirty-three year span of time than at any other time in history. So, Jesus was called a glutton, a winebibber, a blasphemer, an insurrectionist, a partner of Beelzebub, and even insane.

It is hard to keep going, to keep serving God, when you are doing your best and people criticize you for it, especially when the critics are doing nothing themselves. But the true servant of God should expect such. This has always been one of Satan's favorite devices for discouraging us and diverting us. If he can get us listening to people rather than looking to Jesus, he can hinder us.

That's why Jesus taught us, "Blessed are ye, when men shall revile you, and persecute you, and shall say all manner of evil against you falsely, for my sake. Rejoice, and be exceeding glad: for great is your reward in heaven: for so persecuted they the prophets which were before you" (Matt. 5:11-12).

Someone asked Clovis Chappell how he handled criticism. "I have prayed throughout my ministry," he said, "for holy numbness." All who want to remain faithful and true to the Lord need to breathe that same prayer.

We must be careful not to become a part of Satan's blockade against others by having critical spirits. God does not give us the gift of discernment that we might criticize, but that we might intercede. Besides, we will enjoy church more if we don't sit in the seat of the scornful.

The Good Verses the Best

Another blockading tactic of Satan is diversion—getting us to concentrate on secondary matters. A good example of this is found in the Old Testament. A man was captured in battle and committed to another for guarding, but the guard allowed the prisoner to escape. The negligent man explained his failure to perform his duty by saying, "As thy servant was busy here and there, he was gone" (1 Kings 20:40).

Being busy "here and there" has been the downfall of many Christians. We get busy concentrating on secondary matters and neglect those things which are most important. Thus the good in life becomes an enemy of the best.

Nehemiah was called by God to rebuild the walls of the city of Jerusalem. But on every hand obstacles, roadblocks, and difficulties were put in his path. His critics laughed at him and scorned him, saying, "Don't you know that we are in the midst of the greatest economic depression we ever faced and you have just a handful of Jews planning to do this?" They even suggested that a fox could brush against the wall and knock it down.

When derision failed, Nehemiah's critics tried to divert his attention from his main task. They asked him to stop working and discuss the building project with them. Nehemiah refused, saying, "I am doing a great work, so that I cannot come down: why should the work cease, whilst I leave it, and come down to you?" (Neh. 6:3).

Again and again they sought to divert Nehemiah, and every time he responded in the same way. He simply refused to enter into meaningless dialogue that would take him away from his primary mission from God.

If Satan can divert us by getting us to concentrate on secondary matters, he will have accomplished his purpose.

The Golden Wedge of Discouragement

The fourth blockade of Satan is discouragement, attempting to get us so disappointed in ourselves or others that we give up and quit.

The fable is told that the devil once decided that he would retire from business and sell all his diabolical devices. On the day of the sale, all his tools were put on display, each with a price tag.

One rather plain-looking and much-worn tool was priced considerably higher than the others. The devil was asked what it was. "That's the wedge of discouragement," he said.

"Why is it priced so high?"

"Because," the devil answered, "it is more useful to me than all the others. I use it to get into a man's mind, and once inside I can use him to do my work. It is greatly worn because it is my favorite tool. I have used it on nearly everybody, yet few people know that it belongs to me."

Well, according to the fable, the devil's price for discouragement was so high that nobody bought it. And he's still using it.

Satan can take the finest Christian, one who has received Jesus Christ into his life and who is trying to serve Him, and drive the wedge of discouragement into his Christian work and wreck his usefulness. A Sunday School teacher doesn't see the results he wants. A new Christian sees an inconsistent church member. Any good Christian, dead earnest about his work, can become discouraged. Satan can drive the wedge in and pry open a door, and all the rest of his cohorts can go in. He can break a life down with discouragement.

Every Christian needs to be able to cope with discouragement, with criticism, with rejection, with ingratitude, and with periods of barrenness. These can all become Satan's blockades to divert us from the will of God. We must recognize their source. We must identify them as his work and not allow them to stop us.

Elijah became so disappointed and discouraged that he sat down under a juniper tree and wept, hoping to die. Titus became so discouraged at the lack of response in Crete that he asked Paul for a new assignment. It is hard to keep going when the going is hard. The temptation to give up and quit, throw in the towel, walk away saying, "What's the use?" is always before us. We must never get so disappointed in people that we lose our faith in God.

If I were asked to give a motto for the Christian life, it would be this: "Thy will, oh God—nothing more, nothing less, nothing else!" Since the will of God is so important, we must anticipate Satan's opposing it. Obstacles are certain. Roadblocks will come. And when they do, we must recognize their source and surmount them to do the will of God.

6

The Messenger of Satan

One of the most amazing truths in Scripture is that Satan, the adversary of God and of man, sometimes becomes an agent of God in chastening us. What Satan sends to destroy us, God turns to a good purpose and uses it to develop us.

There is an example of this in the life of the apostle Paul. He was facing some stiff opposition in Corinth. His critics not only questioned his apostleship but also boasted of special revelations and visions from God. Paul could have matched them vision for vision and boast for boast, but he refused to do so. He said instead, "If I must needs glory, I will glory in the things which concern mine infirmities" (2 Cor. 11:30).

Then, as though speaking of someone else, Paul told of an experience fourteen years earlier when he had been raptured "to the third heaven" (12:2). He had received such a special revelation from God he could not even talk about it.

In Jewish cosmology there were three heavens. The first heaven was where the birds flew and the clouds floated. The second was where the stars were, the abode of the sun and the moon. The third was where God was. The first heaven was seen by day, the second by night, and the third by faith.

Paul was caught up into the very presence of God. If there were any doubt about Paul's meaning he removed it when he spoke of this as "paradise" (v. 4). The word *paradise* is of Persian origin and means a walled garden. It is the same word Jesus used when He said to the penitent thief on the cross, "To-day shalt thou be with me in paradise" (Luke 23:43). When a Persian king wished to confer a very special honor on someone who was dear to him, he made him *a companion of the garden* and gave him the right to walk in the royal gardens with him in close and intimate fellowship. In this experience, Paul had been a companion of God.

What did Paul see and hear in this experience? He did not say. We only know that he heard "unspeakable words, which it is not lawful for a man to utter." And he never uttered them. If I had such an experience, I couldn't have waited until Sunday morning to tell people about it. But not Paul.

You may ask, "Do you think people have experiences like that today?" Undoubtedly. I'm certain that experiences like that have been granted under certain conditions to certain persons and always with a certain purpose. If people have visions of this sort, they are silent about them. When people want to tell me about their visions, I'm always suspicious. I want to know what they had for supper the night before!

Fourteen years had passed, and Paul had never told about his vision; even when he did speak of it, he did not tell what he had heard. The words were inexplicable and unspeakable, words not lawful for a man to utter. It was a high experience. After simply making reference to his revelation, Paul returned to his original position. He would boast only of his infirmities. He said, "And lest I should be exalted above measure through the abundance

The Messenger of Satan

of the revelations, there was given to me a thorn in the flesh, the messenger of Satan to buffet me, lest I should be exalted above measure" (2 Cor. 12:7).

Paul's great revelation was followed by an experience of darkness of the deepest kind. It was painful, crippling, frustrating, and humiliating. First, he located it. It was "in the flesh." It was not a person who troubled Paul. We sometimes speak of people who distress us as "a thorn in the flesh." But that is not what Paul had in mind. He was talking about a bodily affliction.

What was it? Some believe that it was a form of epilepsy with recurring seizures. Others believe that Paul suffered from chronically recurrent attacks of a certain virulent malaria which haunted the coast of the eastern Mediterranean. One who has suffered from it describes the headache that accompanies it as being like "a red-hot bar thrust through the forehead." Still others believe that Paul suffered from ophthalmia. Paul said of the Galatians that if possible they would have plucked out their eyes and given them to him (Gal. 4:15). Near the end of Galatians he wrote, "See with what large letters I am writing to you" (6:11, NASB), as if he were describing the great sprawling characters that a man who could hardly see would write. We can only speculate about what Paul's thorn in the flesh was.

Paul traced his affliction to its source. He called it a "messenger of Satan." Satan doesn't get nearly as much credit as he deserves in the world today. The Scriptures repeatedly lay the blame for suffering, affliction, and disease at his feet. Job, the great patriarch of the Old Testament, who lost his family, his wealth, and his health was afflicted not by God, but by Satan (Job 2:5-7). Jesus described the woman who had been crippled by a spinal disorder as "one whom Satan hath bound" (Luke 13:16).

And, in his great sermon to Cornelius, Peter described Jesus as "healing all that were oppressed of the devil" (Acts 10:38). Satan, our accuser and our tempter, the deceiver and the divider, the hinderer and the binder, is also the afflictor.

Why did Satan do this to Paul? What was Satan's purpose? Paul said that it was "to buffet" him. The word *buffet* literally means "to strike with the fist." It describes what the Roman soldiers did to Jesus at His trial. They slapped Him, punched Him with their fists. The effect of Paul's infirmity was that it kept him beaten down, weak, and humiliated.

While Paul's affliction came from Satan, God permitted it. Paul expressed this conviction by saying that his thorn in the flesh "was given" to him. The passive tense of the verb refers to God as the Giver.

Nothing comes into our lives unless it first passes through the loving hands of God. Though it comes from Satan, God allows it. And nothing can come unless it is for a purpose. Satan is pictured merely as an agent of God's eternal purposes.

Paul saw that a divine purpose had been worked out through the physical ailment he suffered. It kept him from the pride and arrogance he might have felt because of his special visions. It was a "gift" from God in order to deflate his tendency toward pride. Paul needed some reminder that, in spite of his rapture into heaven, he still was man among men.

Here, as in some other passages, we get the idea that humility was not an easy and automatic virtue for Paul. He could see that the hard and continual discipline of pain and ill health was God's way of saving him from pride that is fatal to the Christian's spirit of usefulness. This is not to say that Paul had a morbid sentimentality toward disease.

The Messenger of Satan

He saw it as an evil thing, the messenger of Satan sent to harass him. God does not want us to suffer sickness or disease. Disease is a blight on His creation, part of the opposition to His creative purpose for His children. But sickness does not come without God's permission.

Three times Paul asked the Lord to take away this affliction, but the Lord's answer was a rich, positive, no. He did, however, promise that He would give Paul grace, unfailing strength, that would enable him to endure it. God would never impose a heavier burden than Paul could bear, for He would always be present to help bear the load. Divine power is always unfailing and invincible. That was God's promise to Paul. It is also His promise to us.

Paul, therefore, vowed that he would "glory" or boast of his infirmity. He would take pleasure in sicknesses, opposition, persecution, and hardships if they came for Christ's sake. For, as he became weak physically, it made him strong spiritually.

This is neither stoicism nor submission to a dispensation of God which is not understood. It is the language of the man who realized that things he desired to escape from were allies of the soul, "lest I should be exalted above measure." Does that seem a weak reason? It is not. There is nothing more hindering to the work of God than the uplifted and proud Christian. Paul thanked God for denying his request. Paul found out that the denial was a loving denial. Thus, God gave him something better than he asked for. He gave Paul grace to serve effectively in spite of his weakness. That's why Paul vowed to "glory" in and "take pleasure" in them. What a marvelous response by Paul. This is always the key to making the most of any experience.

Could Paul have looked upon his thorn as a gift at the

moment? Certainly not, he begged to have it taken away. But fourteen years passed. Through the process of years, Paul understood the Lord's words, "My grace is sufficient for thee" (v. 9).

This whole passage introduces to us the subject of chastisement. In order to discipline us, to teach us, to correct us, to save us, and to make us more useful in His kingdom, God allows Satan to afflict us.

This is at least *one* explanation for the suffering of Christians. When troubles come to us, they are usually either from Satan to discourage us or allowed by God to discipline us. What Satan would use to destroy us, God uses to develop us. The profound truth of this passage is that our adversary can become God's agent to develop us into what we ought to be.

We should learn at least three lessons about chastisement from Paul's experience. First, chastisement is an expression of God's love. Second, the value of chastisement depends upon our response to it. And third, it sometimes takes the passage of time to see the good of an experience.

Whom the Lord Loveth He Chasteneth

Chastisement is an expression of God's love. Paul said the thorn "was given" him; and the word "given" suggests that there is a loving will behind it. If it did not come directly from God's hand, it came through His hand. Jesus referred to His suffering as "the cup which my Father hath given me" (John 18:11). Obviously, the cup had been prepared by human hate, but God had taken it and put it into Jesus' hands for Him to drink.

No matter how suffering comes, we may take it from the loving hands of God, knowing it can be used for our good. We are not at the mercy of divine fate but are always in the hands of a loving God.

The Scriptures make it clear that chastening is an act of love. Solomon wrote, and the writer of Hebrews confirms, "My son, despise not the chastening of the Lord; neither be weary of his correction: For whom the Lord loveth he corrected; even as a father the son in whom he delighteth" (Prov. 3:11-12; also see Heb. 12:5-6).

Satan comes in chastisement to buffet our minds by asking, "How could God do this to you if He really loved you?" The truth is, How could He do otherwise if He loves us? Chastisement is not a denial of God's love but a confirmation of it.

God is our Heavenly Father. Like any good father, He chastens His children to teach them, train them, mature them. If God never chastens us, it is a sure sign that we are not His. Chastisement is one of the practical proofs that we are the sons of God (Heb. 12:8). A father who loves his child will not allow him to do wrong without correction. The responsibilities of fatherhood are great. They are more than biological. They are also moral and spiritual.

How do you envision the love of God? If you see it as soft, permissive, and sentimental, you do not understand it at all. God's love is tough love. It is strict and demanding. He says to us through chastisement, "I love you too much to let you go on in your sin. I will not let you ruin your life." God's chastisement is a measure of how much He loves us.

God is at work in the world. His purpose is not that we might be comfortable, healthy, or prosperous. It is that we might become like His Son, Jesus Christ. In order to accomplish that, God often finds it necessary to chasten us; when He does, it is an act of love.

Our Response Makes the Difference

The value of chastisement is determined by our response to it. What was Paul's response to this thorn in the flesh? He gloried in it and he took a pleasure in it. Why? Because it kept him humbled and dependent on Christ, who was his real strength.

Paul's experience teaches us that what happens "in us" is far more important than what happens "to us." If we respond to chastisement in the right way, we are drawn closer to the Lord and our spiritual lives are enriched. If not, we are impoverished.

I have a friend who went bankrupt several years ago. By his own testimony before that experience he was about the most carnal Christian a person could be. He said, "I hadn't prayed but three times in my adult life. When I got married, I prayed, 'God bless my marriage.' When my first child was about to be born, I prayed, 'God, help my child to be healthy.' And when I was thinking about buying my business, I prayed, 'God, help me get this business.' I didn't want God to help me run it. I could do that by myself. I just wanted Him to help me get it. Then I went broke. From that failure God taught me a lesson I never could have learned any other way."

I have followed that man's life the past ten years. He has grown into one of the most faithful, committed Christians I know because he made the right response to his setback.

Life is a grindstone. Whether it grinds us down or polishes us up depends on our response to our problems. If we respond with reverence, respect, and repentence, we become better. If not, we become bitter.

Some people go broke in business and become sour and resentful toward God. But this man responded in the right way and his adversity was used to make him into a better person. The same can happen to you. That's why the Lord tells us, "My son, despise not thou the chastening of the Lord, nor faint when thou art rebuked of him" (Heb. 12:5).

It Takes Time

Often the passage of time is necessary before we can see the good of an experience. An old Chinese man owned a beautiful stallion. One day the horse broke out of the corral and ran away. A neighbor saw what happened and said to the man, "Oh, that is bad."

The Chinese man said, "I don't know about that. It may be too soon to say."

Two or three days later the stallion came back with a dozen wild horses following him, and he led them into the corral. When the friend heard of this, he said to the man, "That's wonderful. You once had only one horse and now you have thirteen."

Again the Chinese man said, "I don't know about that. It may be too soon to say."

The next day the man's boy was trying to break the wild horses and was thrown off. He broke his leg.

His friend heard about it and responded, "Oh, that is terrible. Your son will be laid up for many months."

The man replied, "I don't know about that. It may be too soon to say."

The next week a Chinese warlord came through the country, conscripted every able-bodied young man, and took them off to war. He did not take the young man who was laid up with a broken leg.

One of our problems in life is that we judge most things by the moment. We ought not to evaluate our experiences too soon. Chastisement which may be grievous at a moment may turn out for our good. It can eventually yield the fruit of righteousness in our lives (Heb. 12:11).

I have lived long enough to thank God for my troubles. What I thought at one time was the benediction to my ministry actually became the invocation to it. But it took time to see it.

When troubles comes, Satan always accompanies them. He attempts to use adversity to buffet us and to break us. But we shouldn't give him the victory. We should remember that God loves us, even though He allows bad things to happen, and respond to Him in patience and humility. Then we, too, can glory in infirmities and take pleasure in distress.

7

An Angel of Light

Would you know the devil if you met him on the street? "Sure, I would," you reply. "He is a well-formed, healthy male, with a red suit, horns, tail, and a pitchfork in his hand. I would know him anywhere!"

This caricature, of course, does not come from Scripture. The Bible draws no portrait of Satan. It comes rather from a combination of Greek mythology and medieval superstition. But I'm sure it must please Satan immensely that he is envisioned like this. Actually, he is the opposite. Satan is beautiful and alluring beyond anything we can imagine.

The apostle Paul stated this when he wrote, "Satan himself is transformed into an angel of light" (2 Cor. 11:14).

The word translated *angel* is the Greek word *Aggelos* which means "messenger." Paul was saying that Satan is an imposter. He is always transforming himself into a messenger, a preacher of righteousness.

The occasion for this statement was a letter written by the apostle Paul to defend his own apostleship and to expose a group of false prophets who were at work in Corinth. These were arrogant, braggadocious, self-seeking men who preached that Jesus was a mere man and that salvation was by works, not by grace. Both their message and their spirit betrayed their true identity.

These men claimed to be apostles, men of God; in reality, as Paul plainly asserted, they were agents of Satan. They were hypocrites, deceivers, masquerading as apostles of Christ. Paul suggested that we should not be surprised, however, because their master, Satan, does the same thing. He, too, is accustomed to masquerading as a messenger of God to further his base designs.

As Paul wrote those words he recalled how Satan deceived Eve in the Garden by his cunning ways, and he was afraid that something like that might happen to the Corinthian church. In the case of Eve, Satan took the form of a serpent. This was not a crawling, slithering, scaly snake. The snake crawling on its belly was a result of the curse put upon it in the Garden (Gen. 3:14). Evidently he appeared to her as something of grace and beauty, perhaps as a flying serpent whose appearance would be appealing.

There is a basic truth here. Evil never comes to us in the guise of evil; it camouflages itself as good. It is the habit of evil to clothe itself in the colors of righteousness. Temptation always appears in the guise of good; otherwise it would not be a temptation. And Satan always comes to us in masquerade, otherwise, we would not listen to him or follow him. For instance, with regard to alcohol, he appears not as a drunken bum but as a "man of distinction." With regard to sex, he assumes the role not of a shameless prostitute, but of a beautiful, popular social butterfly. In the Bible when Satan appears before God, he always appears as Satan. He cannot fool God, for God knows him for who and what he is. But when he appears directly to man, he never appears as Satan. He always assumes some other role, for man does not understand his guile.

An Angel of Light

Satan has many tools. One of his favorites is religious leaders. He delights to come to us as a preacher of righteousness, as a true man of God, and lead us away from the Lord. Just as he masqueraded as a messenger of light in Paul's day, he masquerades as men of God today. This should come as no surprise to us. Jesus himself said, "Take heed that no man deceive you. For many shall come in my name, saying I am the Christ; and shall deceive many" (Matt. 24:4-5). It is the consistent witness of Scripture that the last days will be characterized, more than anything else, by an increase in false prophets and counterfeit religions. Satan's primary tactic is not to build a church and call it "The First Church of Satan." He is far too clever for that. He invades the Sunday School, the seminary classroom, and the pulpit, and he disguises himself as a man of God, a preacher of rightousness.

The devil is a preacher—don't forget it. He is diabolical in his preaching, but he is a preacher. He has another gospel, a substitute Jesus, and another power to perform that which he desires in the lives of men. And his demons are preaching actively. In 1 John 4:1-3, John taught the same thing:

> Believe not every spirit [or teacher] but try the spirits [measure them according to the Word of God. And this is the reason] whether they are of God: because many false prophets are gone out into the world. Hereby know ye the Spirit of God: Every spirit [or teacher] that confesseth that Jesus Christ is come in the flesh is of God: And every spirit that confesseth not that Jesus Christ is come in the flesh is not of God: and this is that spirit of antichrist, whereof ye have heard that it should come; and even now already is it in the world.

It is difficult for us to accept the fact that Satan can use a preacher or a clergyman to proclaim a gospel other than the gospel of Jesus Christ, yet that is often the case today. This does not mean we should be constantly suspicious of every preacher and always looking for heresy in a proud, judgmental way. We should thank God for the thousands of godly men who faithfully proclaim the Scriptures in churches of many different denominations.

At the same time, we must not be naive about Satan's ability to deceive through religion and religious leaders. Satan is an imposter. That has been his tactic since the Garden of Eden and is still his scheme today. His ministers are everywhere masquerading as true men of God, some consciously but still more unconsciously.

How does Satan disguise himself today? What are his favorite masquerades?

Characteristics of Cults

One way Satan disguises himself is through religious cults and cult leaders. It is loosely estimated that some six million Americans belong to more than one thousand religious cults or near-cults.

In the Christian faith, a cult may be defined as a Christian deviation. It is a group that calls itself Christian and uses the Bible and Christian terms but deviates in its theology from basic biblical doctrine as accepted by traditional Christianity. In particular, its deviation centers on the person and work of Jesus Christ but also usually includes the authority of the Bible, the doctrine of God, the Holy Spirit, mankind, and salvation.

There are five characteristics by which we can identify cults.

1. They follow one human leader.
2. They believe in "new" revelations.
3. They dilute the Bible.

4. They take people away from the church.
5. They feed off of the people of God.

Cults always center around a single charismatic leader or authority figure who claims a special relationship with God. Out of that relationship he claims to speak for God as His prophet, apostle, or messiah. He/she is the sole source of revelation from God and the final authority for religious truth. Salvation is attained by accepting the sect leader and his/her teachings.

We all seem to be vulnerable at the point of authority figures. We apparently seem to have a perverse tendency to want to create idols. Whether they are golden calves or Christian superstars, idols are simple and less threatening than the living God. It is easy to embrace what Richard Foster called "the religion of the mediator." If we are not forever careful, we can move quickly and unconsciously into worshiping persons we think to be God's servants instead of God.

One way to spot a false authority figure is to observe how he responds to questions and differences of opinion. The one thing a false messiah hates most is disloyalty. He considers differences of opinions as infidelity. He is not interested in our questions; he wants absolute loyalty. He wants power over the lives of his followers. Hold as suspect any authority figure who does not welcome honest questions and will not answer them frankly.

Acceptance of new teachings from God is another key cultic characteristic. The idea that God and His truth can be found only through the sect leader is coupled with a belief in progressive or supplemental revelations. These new revelations or insights supersede, contradict, or radically reinterpret biblical teachings.

A third characteristic of a sect is the acceptance of new written authority. False religions often ignore or even deny the full inspiration and authority of the Bible as the Word of God. Instead, they substitute other books or a set of teachings that are not based on the Bible. These supersede the Bible or are necessary to interpret the Bible correctly.

The fourth characteristic of a cult is the belief that it is the one true church. With the acceptance of a modern prophetic figure, new revelations from God, and possession of the correct interpretation of the Bible, the cult claims it is the one true church on earth. Coupled with its claim is the teaching that the New Testament church ceased to exist in the earliest Christian centuries, but the true church has been restored to the earth by God through the cult's living leader. Cults teach that God has rejected traditional Christianity as the true faith and chosen the cult as the true church. They alone have the whole truth and, therefore, strongly discourage their members from participating in the worship and instruction of a Christian church; they may even take violent measures to prevent it.

Fifth, cults feed off the people of God. They don't go out and win new converts from among the lost. Rather, they proselyte among those already churched. Like the Pharisee of Jesus' day they compass land and sea to make one proselyte, and, when he is made, he is twofold more a child of hell than they are (see Matt. 23:15).

Don't be deceived. No human leader, no church, no cult can save you from your sins and reconcile you to God. Only Christ can do that—and He will for all who turn to Him in simple faith and place trust in Him as Lord and Savior. The apostle Peter summarized the consistent message of the New Testament from beginning to end: "There is salvation in no one else, for there is no other

An Angel of Light

name under heaven given among men by which we must be saved" (Acts 4:12, RSV; see John 14:6).

And when God gave His truth in Scripture He did not leave us the option of some new revelation later on. The Bible is a complete document from God to us. It does not leave room for supplemental chapters.

When someone adds to or subtracts from God's Word, insists on another book or teacher in order to understand the Bible, or discovers a new theology hidden for generations, don't believe him/her. The Christian faith has been given to us "once and for all" and allows for no additions or subtractions (Jude 3). As Spurgeon said, "There is no new theology unless it is false."

The church is not perfect, and some within the church have even departed from the basic truths of the Christian faith. But God still has His people, and the church is essential to His plan. It is His instrument for world redemption. Hold as suspect any person or group that speaks against His church and insists that they alone have the truth.

I caution you not to believe every religious person who calls on you, no matter how sincere he may seem or how religious he may sound. Test both his message and his spirit by the Word of God. He may be a minister of Satan transformed into an angel of light. He may be a wolf in sheep's clothing.

Watch Out for Heresies

Cult leaders and gurus are relatively easy to identify. Perhaps our greatest danger comes not from them but from what I call "near-cults" or "Christian heresies."

"A heretic," someone has said, "is a person who has a complete grasp of a half-truth." The closer a false teacher gets to the truth, the more dangerous he becomes. Such false prophets are everywhere. They are nothing more than masqueraders sometimes coming into your home on TV, radio, through literature, or, rarely, in person.

These "near-cult" leaders are characterized by three things.

First, they claim to have special visitations from Jesus and from His angels who personally appear to them and talk to them. In these supposed visitations they don't receive new theology but new projects or missions they want us to help them do.

Beware of any one who says to you, "The Lord showed me very clearly . . ." or "Jesus visited and talked to me and told me to . . ." Be suspicious, for these sound more like hallucinations than revelations. They are born out of that messiah complex I have already talked about. I have been a pastor for over thirty years, and in all those years I have been led, directed, and impressed by God again and again, but I have never had a heavenly visitation from Jesus or an angel, nor do I need one. In our church we have built multiple buildings and undertaken vast missions projects, but the Lord never visited me and told me to do any of them. I just looked out and saw the need, prayed about it until I felt God's leading, and then said to my congregation, "Let's do it." God gave me intelligence, and I assume He expects me to use it.

On the surface it may appear to be more spiritual to seek heavenly visitations for all of our decisions rather than just to go ahead and use the intelligence God gave us and do the obvious. But it is not. If God gave you a watch, would you honor him more by asking him for the time of day or by consulting the watch? If God gave a sailor a compass, would the sailor please God more by kneeling in a frenzy of prayer to persuade God to show him which way to go or by steering according to the compass? Except for those things that are specifically commanded or forbidden, it is God's will that we be free to exercise our own intelligent choices.

Suspect Giving

A second thing that characterizes these "near-cult" leaders is their preoccupation with money. They are forever facing an impending financial crisis and will have to go off the air if your gift does not come in immediately.

Recently at least three Better Business Bureaus in Canada found it necessary to alert the public, especially the elderly, to high-pressure financial appeals made by one such television preacher. One of his "faith-building" letters contained a packet of vegetable oil which the evangelist described as "Holy Bible anointing oil." The letter stated that the oil was to be used "to turn God's healing and prospering blessings on in your life." Recipients were told to make a cross on their forehead with the oil; then by faith go into a room alone and take out any money they had and make a cross on each bill. They were told to do this in faith for God to heal their money problems. "Anoint your checkbook if you have one." Finally, his letter asked his supporters to mail the largest bills (currency) or check they had.

In his letters he urged, "Give God your best, then expect His best." "Remember," he wrote, "the greater the sacrifice, the greater the blessing."

Another such TV preacher wrote: "Your seed-faith gift will help you get a hundredfold return," and "God has promised specific increases in the lives of those who help build and equip the research tower."

Their "seed-faith" theology always promises material rewards for sacrificial gifts.

I believe in the law of sowing and reaping, but we can't barter with God. Seed-faith theology, taken to extremes, reduces God to a "sugar daddy"; if you want His blessings and His love, you pay Him off.

If we give to God because we think that by giving we have somehow placed Him in our debt and He is required to come through for us and meet our needs, we have perverted the Scriptures. Our only motive for giving should be love. When we encourage people to give in order to have their needs met or so they will receive "a hundredfold in return," we have appealed to their sense of greed and desperation, neither of which seems admirable to me.

To give correctly we must give out of a pure heart, out of love and thanksgiving. We must give expecting nothing and hoping for nothing in return but God's smile.

While these preachers appeal for our sacrificial gifts, they often build vast personal and financial empires for themselves and their families. Have you noticed they almost all include their sons in their ministry? The reason is, there is no success without a successor. And all the while they live a "jet-set" life-style. They live in expensive homes, drive foreign luxury cars, dress in the finest tailor-made clothing, own elegant winter and summer homes, belong to the most elite country clubs, and enjoy lengthy vacations. In the words of the former daughter-in-law of one of them, "We were allowed great personal excesses."

While the Scriptures teach that the laborer is worthy of his hire and it is not wrong to receive pay, beware of those who promise rewards for sacrificial giving. Don't be hoodwinked into giving God's money to those whose life-style cannot be observed or who give no accounting of their finances to a responsible body. These are often religious con artists who fleece people in the name of God. Those who are preoccupied with money and those who use sophisticated marketing techniques to sell Jesus, to make

Him more attractive so people will become involved and support what they are doing, do not bear the marks of genuine followers of Christ. Like the false prophets of old they "make merchandise" of the innocent and unsuspecting for personal gain (2 Pet. 2:3).

Faith Healing and Faith Healers

Third, these "near-cult" leaders promise health as well as wealth to their followers. They preach that New Testament miracles are still operative and that if their followers will turn to God in faith, He will heal them of all their diseases. But, of course, they never leave themselves unprotected. If you pray and are not healed, then it is because of an insufficient faith on your part! That troubles me. Why does it take so little faith to be saved and so much faith to be healed?

I believe in faith healing, but I do not believe in faith healers (i.e., specially anointed men or women who heal by their touch and their prayer). That day has passed away. Today the ministry of healing has been given to the local church. "Is any sick among you? let him call for the elders of the church; and let them pray over him, anointing him with oil in the name of the Lord: And the prayer of faith shall save the sick, and the Lord shall raise him up" (Jas. 5:14-15*b*).

Beware of any person who claims to have miracle-working power. Oh, I know what they say. "It is God who does the healing." But it is always connected with their touch, their prayers, or some contact with them.

Don't be hoodwinked by those who offer easy solutions to life's problems. The God of the Bible does not promise to change our circumstances but to go through them with us. David expressed it like this, "Yea, though I walk through the valley of the shadow of death, I will fear no evil: for thou art with me; thy rod and thy staff they comfort me" (Ps. 23:4).

We need a better understanding of miracles today. So far as we know from Scripture, Jesus never used any of the people He healed. Those He cured disappeared as soon as He performed His miracles on them. He restored sight to Bartimaeus, who then vanished, to be heard from no more. He raised Jairus's daughter from the dead, and she then promptly faded from the pages of Scripture. He cured the woman who had been crippled for eighteen years, and she then disappeared forever.

On the other hand Jesus did no miracles in the lives of the twelve apostles, but they are the ones He used extensively in doing God's work.

There is no law in Scripture that says God won't use you if He performs a miracle in your life, but He didn't use such people in the days of His flesh. The choice seems to be: Do you want to be used or do you want a miracle?

The point of this chapter is this: There were false prophets masquerading as servants of God in Paul's day and there are false prophets still doing the same thing today. This should not surprise us, for this has long been one of Satan's tactics.

How to Know the Counterfeits

With so many varied religious groups, cults, near cults, and heresies today, we can't know them all.

How, then, can we discern the true from the false?

Billy Graham tells that his wife, Ruth, sat at a banquet one evening with the head of Scotland Yard's counterfeit investigation division. As they talked, she asked him if he did not spend a great deal of time studying counterfeit bills. The inspector replied, "Quite to the contrary. I spend my time studying the real." That way, when he saw a phony, a counterfeit bill, he could spot it immediately.

The best advice against deception I can give is: I urge you to spend your time getting to know Christ and His word. When you know the real, you can more easily spot the counterfeit!

8

The Device of Divisiveness

In one of his speeches on the requisites for military success General Douglas MacArthur placed more emphasis on having a knowledge of the enemy than on anything else. He said, "The greater the knowledge of the enemy, the greater potential of victory." Then, beginning with Joshua and ending with the North African campaign of World War II where Rommel was finally defeated because of the successful work of counterespionage, he traced this principle throughout military history.

This is a principle that has its parallel in the spiritual warfare. The more we know our enemy the better our chances of victory over him. The apostle Paul had this fact in mind when he urged that we forgive one another and be reconciled to one another, "lest Satan should get an advantage of us: for we are not ignorant of his devices" (2 Cor. 2:11). The word for *device* in the Greek means "strategies" or "plans of attack." We must know Satan's "methods of operation" if we hope to win in the spiritual warfare.

Satan might get to us in a hundred ways. He could get to us through doctrinal compromise, through discouragement, through moral impurity, and by getting us to concentrate on secondary goals. But divisiveness is Satan's favorite device. I want you to see him for who he really is. He is not just the accuser, the tempter and the deceiver; he is also the great divider. A quick glance down the pages of church history confirms this fact. Divisiveness diverts us from our main task. We expend our best energies on second-rate causes—on infighting rather than on advancing the kingdom of God. And second, it divides us from one another and, thus, from God. If Satan can get us out of fellowship with one another, he gets us out of fellowship with God, for the two are inseparable.

These words from Paul echo of trouble and of unhappiness. When he visited Corinth, a man organized opposition against him. Paul's short, unhappy visit to the church had been poisoned by the activity of one man. This man had clearly personally insulted Paul. And Paul insisted that discipline be exercised upon him. The majority of Christians had come to see that this man's conduct had not only hurt Paul but also had injured the honor and the good name of the whole Christian church. So discipline had been exercised and the man had repented.

But, obviously, some members in the church felt that the discipline had not been sufficiently severe and desired to take sterner measures and to impose greater punishment on the man. Some people won't let a person change. They never forgive, and they never forget. They think that an offender should pay for a wrong forever.

Paul's plea was that quite enough had been done. The man was now penitent, and to exercise still further discipline would have done far more harm than good. The offender was not to be allowed to despair utterly and to be left to drift away. Since he had repented, he was to be brought back into the church fellowship. So Paul pleaded for mercy on the man who had been his enemy saying, in effect: "I forgive the man, now you forgive him also."

Then he added this postscript, "Lest Satan should get an advantage of us; for we are not ignorant of his devices."

If an unforgiving spirit is kept after the offender has repented, only Satan will benefit. He will find a beachhead to land in our lives and do greater harm. This is ever and always one of Satan's favorite strategies—to get us out of fellowship with one another. If we get out of fellowship with one another, we are out of fellowship with God. Then Satan has the upper hand.

Hurts come to all of us. They are inevitable in life. So the need for forgiveness is continual: you are falsely accused by an employer or a teacher and your faith in justice and authority dies; you are betrayed by your closest friend, the person you trusted the most; your husband leaves you for another woman; you make a mistake and somebody rubs it in too deep, insulting you, poking fun at your business ability, your intelligence, your manners or taste. Or a Christian brother disappoints you, which can be one of the deepest of all hurts. These and many other occasions call for forgiveness in our lives. These things can all leave deep scars on our souls.

When people hurt us our first inclination is to try to get even. We want to pay them back, "an eye for an eye, a tooth for a tooth," serve them their own sauce.

If any conviction about such things comes naturally to all people, it is the deep-seated, universal belief that "somebody has to pay." Why shouldn't the people who have wronged us be made to "make things right"—to pay for their wrongs?

If we don't try to get even, we nurse a grudge until it grows into full-blown hate—hooves, horns, tail, and all. If we don't actually retaliate and seek revenge, we can have the soul satisfaction of reliving the hurt again and again, constantly reviewing, rehashing our old grievances.

To forgive never comes easy; it is the hardest thing in the universe. What is forgiveness? It is not just tolerance or make-believe; it is not a game of winking at hurts. It is something much, much deeper.

The verb "forgive" that Paul used in verse 7 is the Greek word *charizomai*, which means "to pardon" or "to give freely or graciously as a favor." Forgiveness is always something we give; it is not something a person earns or pays for. If offenders have to pay, it is not forgiveness. When we forgive others, we freely pardon their wrong. We pay for it and don't try to make them pay or try to get even.

Forgiveness denies the self that demands its "rights." It repudiates open revenge. It refuses to try to get the other person "back." Instead, it chooses to hurt, to suffer; that is one of the hardest voluntary choices anyone can make —to accept undeserved suffering, suffering that could have been avoided, suffering that rightfully belonged to the offender.

Let me illustrate. Suppose I break a priceless vase that you treasure, and you forgive me? You bear the loss, and I go free. Or, suppose I break your heart? If you forgive me, you must suffer the consequences of my sin, and I go free.

All forgiveness, human and divine, is by its very nature substitutional. No one ever really forgives another except he bears the penalty of the other's sin against him.

This substitution was perfectly expressed in Jesus Christ, who tasted death for all people (Heb. 2:9). He substituted Himself for us, bearing the wrath, the indignation of our sin while we go free. That's what forgiveness cost! Now we must forgive others just as Christ has forgiven us (Col. 3:13; Eph. 4:32). We must bear the cost of forgiving others just as God did for us.

The Device of Divisiveness

"But," you say, "I can't forgive. I have been too deeply hurt. I just can't do it." Yes, yes, you can! Forgiveness is always a choice. No matter what has been done against you, no matter what hurt has been inflicted, you can forgive. Not only can we, we must!

You must do it for your physical and emotional and spiritual well-being. Harbored hatred and unforgiveness can elevate blood pressure, upset the digestive system, ulcerate a stomach, or bring on a nervous breakdown. Have you ever heard of a coronary? The man who broods over wrong poisons his own soul. Boiling inside is a form of slow suicide.

Doctor Loring T. Swaim, a former president of the American Medical Association, wrote a book entitled *Arthritis, Medicine, and the Spiritual Laws*. From long observation Dr. Swaim became convinced that arthritis often stems from chronic resentment or hate. He gives many examples of arthritics being cured once patients overcome their hostile feelings. Medical professionals generally accept that anger, resentment, and unresolved hostilities are principal factors in depression and other emotional disorders.

The spiritual consequences of unforgiveness are equally serious. If Satan can keep us from forgiving others, if he can cause us to hate, to resent, he separates us from one another. When he separates us from one another, he has separated us from God. There is no such thing as being right with God and wrong with our fellowman. We cannot be out of fellowship with our brother and in fellowship with our Father. It is just not possible. So when we do not forgive, we give Satan the upper hand in our lives. Through it he interrupts our worship, prevents our forgiveness, and hinders our prayers. This makes exercising forgiveness more than a recommendation; It is a must.

After the fall of Adam and Eve, Satan wasted no time in showing how he would use jealousy, anger, and hate to accomplish his purposes. The first man to discover the explosive power of these emotions was Cain, the first mortal man born in this world.

That explosion was ignited by jealousy. Cain just couldn't take the fact that God accepted the sacrifice of his kid brother, Abel, and rejected his own. Jealousy flamed to anger, anger to hatred, hatred to murder. The story is told in Genesis 4.

> So Cain was very angry, and his countenance fell. The Lord said to Cain, "Why are you angry and why has your countenance fallen? If you do well, will you not be accepted? And if you do not well, sin is couching [like a lion] at your door; its desire is for you, but you must master it" (Gen. 4:6-7, RSV).

This, the first recorded conversation between a procreated man and God, is amazingly a word of warning about the dangers of anger.

"Look out," God said to Cain. "Sin lurks outside your door as a lion lying in wait. Master the monster of evil, or it will master you." That is it: Right at the beginning, primeval man had his first brush with sin. It was the plummeting fall of man totally blind to the well-muscled malice that swiftly and surely was mastering his heart.

Since the first murder ocurred over worship, it is not surprising that the Lord said, "If therefore you are presenting your offering at the altar, and there remember that your brother has something against you, leave your offering there before the altar and go your way; first be reconciled to your brother and then come and present your offering" (Matt. 5:23-24, NASB).

Here is a principle of worship that we dare not miss: Man's spirit is of utmost importance to God. We cannot worship the Father and hate our brother at the same time. Unforgiveness becomes a device of Satan to cut us off from worship. And when he cuts us off from worship, we lose our spiritual vitality and soon slip into other sins. Paul spoke succinctly about anger when he wrote, "Be angry, and yet do not sin; do not let the sun go down on your anger, and do not give the devil an opportunity" (Eph. 4:26-27, NASB).

I see three important things in these verses. The first is simple and clear. Anger is not an evil in itself; it is a God-given emotion. Paul said, "Be angry, and yet do not sin." Not every expression of anger is wrong. Everyone gets angry occasionally. It is a perfectly normal and healthy emotion.

Second, don't let anger and resentments accumulate. Anger is to be handled on a daily basis. Each new day will have a dark cloud if one enters it encumbered with the smelly garbage of yesterday's anger. Dealing with anger as soon as possible is the only way to keep it from growing and spreading like a poison throughout one's entire life, developing into deep-seated resentments and bitterness.

I believe this is to be taken very literally. Don't let sin come in by prolonging your anger. Paul's advice is, "Simmer down before sundown!"

Third, anger is just one letter short of danger. "Don't give the devil an opportunity," Paul warned (v. 27, NASB). When we allow anger to be expressed in harmful, detrimental ways, we are weakened and the devil reproduces his character through us. When we allow anger to turn into rage, we give Satan a foothold in our lives.

Near the beginning of the play *Julius Caesar,* before

Caesar's assassination, Casca had a premonition of disaster that he reported to Cicero: "Against the Capitol I met a lion, Who glared upon me, and went surly by." The implication is that in every civilization, however lofty, a lion always roams the streets; the jungle never entirely disappears. When anger is uncontrolled, we give place to the lion within our souls.

Anger is one of the most difficult emotions to handle. We can't keep from becoming angry. Anger is the natural response to provocation. However, even though we can't keep from being angry, we can choose how we will handle it. When we realize we are angry, we have a split second in which to decide how to respond. We must determine never to express anger in harmful, detrimental ways. One of Peter's less famous principles goes like this: "Speak when you are angry—and you'll make the best speech you'll ever regret." Anger is like a two-edged sword which can be used to injure both oneself and others—or it can be used constructively and creatively.

A Luxury We Cannot Afford

We must forgive because the lack of it prevents our own forgiveness from God. Jesus said, "For if you forgive men their trespasses, your heavenly Father also will forgive you; but if you do not forgive men their trespasses, neither your Father will forgive your trespasses" (Matt. 6:14-15, RSV).

Only if we have no need for forgiveness ourselves do we dare consider hesitating to forgive another.

"I never forgive," General James Oglethorpe said to John Wesley.

"Then I hope, Sir," replied Wesley, "you never sin!"

We do need forgiveness constantly, don't we? Yes, we need forgiveness of our fellowmen and, far more seriously, the forgiveness of God. Those two go hand in hand. They interlock. They cannot be separated.

Any person who refuses to forgive will not be forgiven because she has cut herself off from love and mercy. She destroys the bridge over which she must travel. But the person who forgives opens her life to the free, gracious forgiveness of her Lord. To be forgiven of God for our trespasses we must forgive, accept, and love.

The person who loves God must also love his neighbor. He who hates his brother does not and cannot love God. Love of God and of man are interlocking and indivisible. Since Jesus said this is true, forgiving and being forgiven forms the one crucial, central, and eternal matter of every life. An unforgiving heart is unforgivable.

Nothing people can do to us can in any way compare with what we have done to God nor what we continue to do to Him, day by day! Since God has forgiven us the debt we owe Him, how can we then be unforgiving to others who owe us so little in comparison? Anything we may need to forgive is only a shadow of the debt we have been forgiven.

The Lord gave instructions for being reconciled to an offender:

1. Go and see him in private. Tell him, not somebody else.

2. If he does not listen, take two or three others with you. Perhaps they can arbitrate between you.

3. If he refuses to listen to them, tell it to the church. It is the ultimate court of appeals for believers.

4. If he refuses to listen even to the church, let him be to you as a heathen (Matt. 18:15-17).

Static on the Prayer Line

A third reason we must forgive is that quarreling and contention hinder our prayer life. Peter admonished husbands and wives to be understanding and considerate of one another, to live in a harmonious relationship, "that [their] prayers be not hindered" (1 Pet. 3:7).

The word "hindered" means "interrupted." Strife in the home is like static on a radio; it interferes with proper reception. A quarreling couple will hardly be a praying one. The static of their relationship will make their prayers ineffective.

I do not know of anything that will alter our life more than meeting God in daily prayer. Prayer is the heart of a personal relationship with God. Ultimately, we have no spiritual life without prayer. Unless we meet God in prayer, we do not meet Him at all.

What is prayer? Prayer is not a blank check signed by our heavenly grandfather. Nor is it a magic charm, such as a rabbit's foot or an Aladdin's lamp. Prayer is conversation, a loving dialogue, with the one who knows us best and loves us most—our Heavenly Father.

We must talk to people in order to get to know them. So, we do not pray just to get things from God. We pray to get to know God Himself. We can know about God without prayer, but prayer is our one way of knowing Him.

Contention, anger, and unforgiveness put static on the prayer line, and the message cannot get through. Divisiveness is one of Satan's best devices. If he can get us out of harmony with one another, he can keep us out of harmony with God.

You may be wondering, *How can I forgive? How can I forgive when the cost is staggering, the pain unbearable, the resentment still swelling?* You can't, alone, It's too hard. You'll need the strength to love and forgive that you can absorb only from God. You will need all the potency of prayer, all the power of His compassion within you, and all the cooperation of His healing touch that you can muster. You see, it takes two to work through this matter of forgiveness—God and you. The secret is God's working it in and your working it out in life. He works within you; you work it out in heart and mind.

How can I forgive? May I suggest prayer? It has potency beyond what most people understand. Have you prayed with a forgiving heart for the person who did you wrong? You cannot hate anyone you pray for regularly; you cannot!

You can forgive by the power of the indwelling Holy Spirit. When you are dominated by self and sin, you cannot forgive. But when you allow the Holy Spirit to work through you, you can forgive.

We need to pray with the psalmist, "Create in me a clean heart, O, God; and renew a right spirit within me" (Ps. 51:10).

Open your life totally to Christ. As you know Him more clearly, follow Him more nearly, love Him more dearly, then forgiving love will be yours.

In writing to the church at Ephesus, Paul challenged Christians: "Be kind one to another, tender-hearted, forgiving each other, just as God in Christ also has forgiven you" (4:32, NASB).

If God forgave us because of Jesus Christ, for the same reason we, too, can and must forgive others.

9

The Binding of Satan

I remember the first time I heard someone talk about rebuking Satan and taking authority over him. It was in a prayer that went something like this: "Satan, we rebuke you. In the strong name of Jesus Christ, we take authority over you and bind you from this place."

When I heard that prayer, I thought, *That's not right. You can't do that, you can't bind Satan.* I reasoned, *If you can bind Satan from a place of worship simply by praying, why not bind him from the whole city? If you can bind him from the whole city, why not bind him from the whole state? If you can bind him from the whole state, why not bind him from the whole nation? If you can bind him from the whole nation, why not bind him from the whole world?*

But reason is not the final authority in the Christian life. Revelation is. So I went to the Scriptures to see what they had to say. I found in them absolutely no support, not one word of encouragement that we could bind Satan from any place. We are told to "resist" Satan and to "withstand" him, but we are never told that we can bind him.

Satan will be bound at the end of time. John, in the Revelation, wrote, "And I saw an angel come down from heaven, having the key of the bottomless pit and a great chain in his hand. And he laid hold on the dragon, that old serpent, which is the Devil, and Satan, and bound him a thousand years" (20:1-2). Satan will be bound at the end of time. But, in the meantime, he "as a roaring lion, walketh about, seeking whom he may devour" (1 Pet. 5:8).

Beyond that, the only binding of Satan talked about in Scripture is that which he does. The truth is, we cannot bind Satan but he can bind us. In fact that is one of his principal works. Thus far we have seen him as the accuser, the slanderer, the tempter, the liar, the deceiver, the divider, and the hinderer. Now I want to look at him as the binder.

An experience from the life of Jesus teaches us this that Satan is the binder (Luke 13:11-17). As was Jesus' custom, He went to the synagogue on the sabbath, and there He found a woman who had had some kind of spinal deformity for eighteen years. Luke, the physician-evangelist, described her as being "bowed together" so that she "could in no wise lift up herself" (v. 11). "Bowed together" is a medical term found nowhere else in the New Testament. It literally means "bent double." And the phrase "lift herself up" is also a medical term. She was bent double and her eyes were always on the ground. She was a pathetic cripple.

When Jesus saw her, He called her to Him and said to her, "Woman, thou art loosed from thine infirmity" (v. 12). He laid His hands on her, and immediately she stood up straight and began to glorify God.

The ruler of the synagogue became indignant because Jesus had healed this woman on the sabbath. The Jewish law permitted helping someone on the sabbath who was in actual danger of his life, but that was not the case here. This healing was considered work. Thus the act of Jesus was, according to Jewish tradition, a violation of the Fourth Commandment: "Six days shalt thou labour, and do all thy work. But the seventh day is the sabbath of the Lord thy God: in it thou shalt not do any work" (Ex. 20:9-10).

The ruler of the synagogue was a narrow-minded bigot. He put his religious traditions above the needs of people. Jesus pointed out that such people found no problem with untying an ox or an ass from its stall and leading it to water on the sabbath day but that they did find fault with His loosing this woman from her infirmity. That was sheer hypocrisy.

Jesus then responded, "Ought not this woman, being a daughter of Abraham, whom Satan hath bound, lo these eighteen years, be loosed from this bond on the sabbath day?" (v. 16).

Mark those words "whom Satan hath bound." They speak to us about the afflicting, crippling, binding work of Satan.

The Source of Sickness

Jesus said that this woman's muscles had been tied in knots by Satan. He was the one who had bound her, crippled her for the past eighteen years. He saw Satan as the source of her affliction.

All of the violence in the world—turbulence of nature, the stresses of the wind and the storm, and the disease that afflicts us—was not intended by God. It is of Satan. We would do well to remember that, for often illnesses, afflictions, and tragedies are blamed on God. This is a prime example of the worldwide deception of Satan.

Second only to the way Satan deceives us concerning his own existence is the way he uses suffering and sorrow to discredit God. Satan is so cunning that he causes the sorrow of our world and God gets the blame. When have you ever heard Satan blamed for tragedy or disaster? It is always the character of God that is called into question when trouble comes. Evil and suffering have placed more question marks on the good name of God than anything else in the world.

If Satan can cause an accident, give a person cancer, or take the life of a little child in order to discredit God and to destroy our faith, he will gladly do it. And when he does nobody ever cries out, "Why has Satan done this to me?" No one ever labels it as an "act of Satan" and no one ever calls it "the will of the devil." Do you see how cunning, how clever he is? He causes most of our troubles, and God gets the blame.

A word of caution, however. This does not mean that this suffering or any person's suffering is necessarily a direct result of personal sin. This woman was a victim of demonic activity that had produced a physical disability, but there is no hint that it was due to sin in her life. As a matter of fact she was in the synagogue when Jesus saw her. She had found her way to the place of worship. There is no reason to believe that this was an unusual experience for her.

When Jesus called her "a daughter of Abraham," he did not merely mean she was a Jewess. He was using the term in its full spiritual significance as revealing her faith in God. Here, then, is a case of physical suffering by a church going woman with a deep faith in God that was directly produced by the power of Satan.

Experiences like this trouble us deeply. We can understand the suffering of evil and wicked people. But the good suffer too. Infants and children suffer, even before they know good from evil. Christians seem to be susceptible to the same maladies as the ungodly. Sickness and suffering are completely indiscriminate. They come to

The Binding of Satan

the rich and to the poor, the young and the old, the good and the bad.

These are mysteries that baffle us. Why was such a thing permitted? How did Satan gain power over this woman? These and many other questions remain unanswered. But the fact remains, a woman—a worshiper, a daughter of Abraham in the full spiritual sense of the word—was bound by Satan, and Christ liberated her.

While we have no final answer as to why one person suffers and another does not, we do know that God has purposes to accomplish in the suffering of His people. He allows suffering as a part of our experience for several reasons:

1. That we might move on to Christian maturity (Jas. 1:2-4; Rom. 8:28-29). God's purpose for each of us is that we might become like His Son, Jesus Christ. To this end He can and does use all things—even the tragedies of life.

2. That we might glorify God (John 9:1-3; 11:4). I have a Christian friend who, at this minute, is dying from cancer. All of her life she has sought to serve the Lord, and for years she has been a faithful Sunday School teacher. She has used her illness as an opportunity to witness. She said to me, "I believe Christians have as much responsibility for the way they die as the way they live."

To that I would add, "We have as much responsibility for the way we suffer as we do for the way we live and the way we die." Through valiant, victorious suffering, we can show Christ's overcoming power to the world and, thus, glorify God.

3. That we might understand that we are simply "earthen vessels" whom God uses for His glory (2 Cor. 12:1-10). Suffering knocks a great amount of nonsense out of us. It reminds us of our weakness, fraility, and total dependence upon Him.

4. That we might be in a position to comfort and encourage other people who are suffering (2 Cor. 1:4-6). If we as God's people never suffered, we could not identify with the vast host of suffering humanity and share with them the comfort we have found in our Lord.

5. That we might long for our glorified bodies and the new Jerusalem (Rom. 8:23; 2 Cor. 5:2; Rev. 21:4). We so easily settle down and become at home in this world. If life were a bed of roses, we might never look longingly toward our heavenly home and point others there also.

In summary, in spite of the fact that suffering comes from Satan, it is a part of God's eternal purpose to conform us to the image of Jesus Christ (Rom. 8:29). This is the "good" toward which God is working all things in our lives (v. 28). We tend to equate *good* with *pleasant* but God does not. *Good* is anything which will make us more like Christ. Suffering is allowed, therefore, by God as a part of His overall plan. While it remains a mystery in many ways, we at least know its source.

The Great Emancipator

Satan had bound this woman, but Jesus liberated her. Infirmities are not, therefore, the will of God. Rather, the woman's crippled condition was a frustration of God's purposes in creation. The whole action of Jesus in this matter makes clear that God does not will for any human being to suffer one moment longer than absolutely necessary.

If Jesus had postponed the healing of this woman until the next day, no one could have criticized Him. After all, she had been crippled for eighteen years. What could one more day matter? But Jesus insisted that suffering must not be allowed to continue until tomorrow if it could be relieved today. So He spoke to her and touched her; in a

The Binding of Satan

moment, she was straight. One of the characteristics of the healing work of Jesus is that it was immediate, complete, and permanent. There was no wondering whether a person were healed when Jesus healed.

This woman had been bound by Satan; Jesus, by a word and a touch, set her free. This demonstrates the power and authority of Jesus over Satan.

Are There Miracles Today?

Jesus had mighty, miracle-working power, and He passed that power on to His apostles. So in the life of the early church, we also find many such wonderful miracles.

The question naturally arises: Do believers have such power today? Are there people who can speak to, pray for, or touch the sick and cause them to be healed as Jesus and the apostles healed?

I don't mean curing people of headaches or sinus or asthma. I mean bona fide miracles. I mean people blind from birth being made to see with perfect twenty-twenty vision. I mean people who have been dead, not for three minutes but for three days, coming back to life again. I mean people who have been helplessly and hopelessly crippled for eighteen years walking again. I mean these people being healed instantaneously, completely, and permanently. Are miracles in the New Testament sense happening today?

You can find a host of TV and radio evangelists on any given Sunday who say yes. They argue that our God is the same God who parted the waters of the Red Sea. He is the same God who sent fire from heaven in the days of Elijah. And the same God who raised Jesus from the dead. Since Jesus is the same yesterday, today, and forever, we can expect the same kind of New Testament miracles to be done today. I agree that our God parted the Red Sea, sent fire from heaven, and raised Jesus from the dead. I believe Jesus is the same yesterday, today, and forever. However, the fact that God is the same does not mean that He works in exactly the same manner in every age.

Biblical history includes three great clusters of miracles (including physical healings): the time of Moses and the Exodus; the time of Elijah and Elisha; and the time of Christ and the apostles. In between these clusters of miracles, years seemed to have passed with no miracles at all.

God led the children of Israel through the wilderness with a pillar of cloud by day and a pillar of fire by night. But has He ever led you that way? He hasn't?

He fed Israel with fresh manna from heaven every day for forty years. Each new day they received a divine care package filled with manna. But, has he ever fed you that way? He hasn't?

As God led Israel through the wilderness, neither their clothes nor their shoes grew old upon them. Do you have a suit or a pair of shoes you have been wearing daily for forty years that has never worn out? You don't?

The Lord once spoke to His prophet Balaam through a walleyed, lop-eared, braying jackass. Has he ever spoken to you through a donkey? He hasn't?

Well, then, God doesn't work in all ages the same way, does He? Jesus came with signs and wonders. He did many mighty miracles. He passed His miracle-working power on to His disciples. They also did miracles and wonders. But He never intended that such miracles should continue.

Paul wrote to the church at Corinth saying that his ministry among them had been marked with the "signs of an apostle" (2 Cor. 12:12). He was referring to the miracles, wonders, and mighty deeds that he did among them.

Some people in Corinth questioned the genuineness of

The Binding of Satan

Paul's apostleship. His defense was, "The signs of an apostle were wrought among you." The miracles, healings, that he performed were evidences that he was a real apostle. Obviously, not everybody could do those miracles; otherwise they would not have been the signs of an apostle. The miracles of Jesus authenticated His messiahship. The miracles of the apostles authenticated their apostleship. They were never intended for all people or for all ages.

This is not to say that miracles do not happen today. They do! God does occasionally heal today in an immediate, direct manner when it is His will to do so. Most of us know of instances of such healings. But contrary to the claims of the modern healing movement, these are exceptional cases and do not represent the norm.

We do not understand why God miraculously heals some and choses not to heal others. We must simply trust a sovereign and loving God who makes no mistakes and "who worketh all things after the counsel of his own will" (Eph. 1:11).

"What are you trying to do, destroy our faith?" you may ask. No, not at all. I am not trying to destroy your faith; I am trying to give you a solid one. I want you to have the kind of faith that will stand the test of adversity.

The apostle Paul expressed the desire "that we henceforth be no more children, tossed to and fro, and carried about with every wind of doctrine" (Eph. 4:14).

The winds of doctrinal confusion are blowing with gale-like ferocity in today's world. And some of the finest, most sincere of God's people are being swept away simply because they do not have a well-grounded faith. Ultimately they are headed for shipwreck because what they believe cannot stand the test of time and experience. The end result is that Satan will win another victory. He conquers some through binding them physically and others through confusing them doctrinally.

While the Lord has not promised to loose everyone who is bound physically by some infirmity, He will loose us from the bondage of sin.

Some of you are bound, not by physical infirmities, but by spiritual ones. You are enslaved by sins that you cannot quit. Alcoholism, drug addition, lust, greed, anger, prejudice, or an uncontrollable temper may have you bound. You may be bent double by your sin so that you cannot look yourself or God in the face. But Jesus, the Great Emancipator, can loose you and cause you to stand tall and straight again. He is stronger than the strong one who has bound you.

10

Victors Instead of Victims

A young football coach was hired as a scout for his college. Before his first assignment, he said, "Coach, what kind of player are you looking for?"

The coach said, "Well, there is the kind of guy who when you knock him down, just stays down."

"We don't want him, do we, Coach?"

"No. Then there is the kind of guy who, when you knock him down, gets up. But if you knock him down the second time, he just stays down."

"We don't want him either, do we, Coach?"

"No, we sure don't. But there is the kind of guy who, when you knock him down, gets up; knock him down, and he gets up; knock him down, and he gets up; knock him down again, and he just keeps getting up every time."

"That's the guy we want; right, Coach?"

"No, we don't want him, either. What I want you to do is find the guy who is knocking all the other guys down. That's the guy I want."

I say amen to that. I'm glad God enables us by His grace to keep getting up and starting over everytime Satan knocks us down.

But it would be better if we could avoid being knocked down in the first place. If we could avoid falling, we wouldn't have to start over again. The Lord holds this promise out to us in Ephesians 6:10-18. "Finally, my brethren, be strong in the Lord and in the power of his might. Put on the whole armour of God, that you may be able to stand against the wiles of the devil" (vv. 10-11). The word "wiles" refers to the devil's devices or crafty methods and suggests his deceitfulness. He is a tested, old warrior who will use any devious means to his advantage.

Paul's words remind us that our warfare is not against mere mortals. "For we wrestle not against flesh and blood, but against principalities, against powers, against the rulers of the darkness of this world, against spiritual wickedness in high places" (v. 12). Our enemy is Satan. He is the opposer of God and His people and the leader of a vast host of evil spirits whose works are organized into a militarylike structure. A hierarchy of spiritual, invisible powers are in rebellion against God under Satan's direction.

Therefore, we are urged, "Take unto you the whole armour of God, that you may be able to withstand in the evil day, and having done all, to stand" (v. 13).

The word "stand" means to "hold your ground, to resist successfully." The phrase, "Put on" in verse 11 and the phrase "take unto you" in verse 13, both denote urgent and decisive action. The idea is that we as believers have been given sufficient equipment to stand our ground against Satan. With that equipment, we are completely adequate to resist him successfully. But we must put it on. We have the option of trying to resist Satan in our own strength or in the Lord's strength. The weapons are ours, but we must avail ourselves of them. We must faithfully accept every instrument and implement that God offers.

By reading the Old Testament, we discover that every saint, every prophet, every patriarch, every one of the glorious kings of Israel was defeated at some time or other by the devil. All of them—the meekest of them, Moses;

the wisest of them, Solomon; the strongest of them, Samson; the greatest of them, David—were absolutely helpless in attempting to outwit Satan by themselves.

But the promise of Scripture is that through the Lord Jesus Christ we can become victors instead of victims. Through Christ we can stand up against Satan, hold our ground, resist him successfully. Paul employed the imagery of a Roman soldier fully equipped for battle to encourage us in the Christian warfare. He asserted that the Christian finds protection in this moral conflict by the use of the whole armor of God and the practice of incessant prayer. Satan loses the battle with us when we learn to stand our ground against him in the grace and strength provided by our Savior.

As Paul compared our resources to a soldier's armor, he used highly figurative language. These are symbols of something real. In order to understand them we must look behind the figure to the reality. What are the spiritual resources God offers for us?

Tested by Sunlight

The first piece of spiritual armor God gives us is the girdle of truth (v. 14). The soldier's girdle was a broad leather belt that served to hold his tunic in place and from which the scabbard for his sword was suspended. "Truth" is without the article in the Greek text and, therefore, carries the idea of sincerity and truthfulness. We will not be successful in resisting and overcoming the evil of Satan if we are hypocritical or dishonest.

Paul's prayer for the Philippian Christians was that they might "be sincere and without offence till the day of Christ" (Phil. 1:10). The word which is used for "sincere" is an interesting word. It literally means "tested by sunlight." It describes that which can be inspected by being held up to the light of the sun without any flaws appearing. It brings to mind the practice of early shoppers for pottery. Often as the potter fired his product, it would crack under the heat of the furnace. Rather than discard the cracked vessel or sell it at a discount, he would press colored wax into the cracks to disguise them and to make the vessel appear perfect. The wise shopper would lift a vessel up to the sunlight and examine it carefully. If there were cracks in it, the sunlight would filter through and reveal them. Paul's prayer is that our character can stand the test of investigation, the test of sunlight, without having flaws in it.

As children of God, we must not merely say that we desire victory over sin; we must truly long for it. Our spiritual vows and public statements must always be sincerely spoken, for the devil has no difficulty in defeating the insincere and half-hearted.

We face an enemy called "the father of lies" (John 8:44, RSV). He is the embodiment of deceit. He likes to be regarded as an angel of light; in reality, he brings despair and darkness and death. Such an enemy can be opposed only by sincerity and truth. If we are deceitful, hypocritical, and insincere, we play into his hands and cannot adequately resist him.

Stay on the King's Highway

Another essential part of the Roman soldier's equipment was the breastplate which, as its name suggests, protected the vital organs in the chest area—heart, lungs, and stomach cavity. Without a breastplate, a warrior was vulnerable to every assault of the enemy. Paul said that righteousness is our breastplate (Eph. 6:14). This righteousness is sometimes understood to be the righteousness of justification, that which Paul elsewhere called "the righteousness which is of God by faith" (Phil. 3:9). We stand in Christ's righteousness, not in our own merits. By grace we are what we are. We stand in His righteousness before God. If we fail in the Christian life, as we do from time to time, our position before God is still secure. It is not based upon the good we've done but Christ's righteousness.

However, a favorite strategy of the devil is to persuade us that we can live as we please since we are fully protected by God. Having been declared righteous by God in Christ, we need to live righteous lives on earth. So, the word "righteousness" represents the believer's way of living. Such righteousness guards our hearts and lives against Satan.

Sin always weakens us. A nail, no matter how small, cannot be driven into a piece of timber, no matter how large, without weakening the lumber some. Likewise, we cannot allow sin, no matter how small, to remain in our lives without weakening our resistance to some degree against the evil one. Believers who desire to ward off the attacks of Satan must consciously choose to be obedient, moral, and devout.

Alfred, the king of the West Saxons, promised safe passage from thieves and robbers on all his highway, as long as the traveler stayed on the road. If the traveler wandered on the moors or out in the woods, there was no assurance of safety. Christians who keep on the King's highway will be safe also.

A Personal Bodyguard

The well-equipped soldier in Paul's day wore sandals with soles thickly studded with hobnails. Such sandals not only gave protection to the feet but also enabled the soldiers, no matter how slippery the ground, to be able to stand firmly and to move quickly and surely because of the cleat-like effect. In ancient times, when warfare was largely a matter of hand-to-hand combat, this surefootedness was essential. The Christian, Paul explained, must have on his feet "the preparation of the gospel of peace" (Eph. 6:15). Most interpreters understand "preparation" to be in the sense of "readiness" to serve God. The idea is that of a disposition of mind that makes men quick to see their duty and ever ready to plunge into the fight. This readiness comes from, or is produced by, "the gospel of peace."

The gospel is designated as the "gospel of peace" because it is a peace-bringing power that destroys the enmity in human hearts and establishes tranquility in its place. This heartpeace produced by the gospel readies the Christian warrior for combat. To have a consciousness of peace with God and to live in tranquil communion with Him enables one to enter into the battle with strong determination and calm assurance.

Wilberforce once said that Christianity could be condensed into four words: *admit, submit, commit,* and *transmit.* The meaning of each of these words is obvious. The gospel leads to peace with God, and the peace of God we are to be ready to share at all times. The believer who does not bear a testimony loses spiritual keenness and becomes vulnerable to Satan's attacks.

The Shield of Faith

Next, Paul named "the shield of faith." This refers not to the small round shield that was carried by cavalrymen but to the large oblong shield that the heavily armed foot soldiers carried. Behind it a man was fully protected. That is the kind of shield, Paul said, that our conflict requires.

"Fiery darts," among the most dangerous weapons used

in ancient warfare, were arrows dipped in pitch or some other combustible material and set on fire before being thrown at the enemy. They not only wounded but also burned. The soldier's best protection—indeed his only real protection—was to manipulate his shield so that these flaming missiles sank into its wood. Thus, the missile was stopped and its fire extinguished.

Faith is our shield. Faith is utter dependence on God. It affords protection for us when we confront Satan's most vicious attacks. We tend to make faith too complicated. It is nothing more and nothing less than believing God when He says that He has done something for us or will do it and then trusting Him to keep His word. It is so simple that it is hard to explain. If anyone asked me what it means to trust another to do a piece of work for me, I could answer only that it means committing the work to that person and leaving it without anxiety in his hands. All of us have many times trusted very important affairs to others in this way and have felt perfect rest in that confidence.

We continually trust our lives, without a thought or fear, to doctors, cooks, taxi drivers, pharmacists, and all sorts of paid servants who have us completely at their mercy and who could, if they chose to do so or if they failed in the necessary carefulness, plunge us into death in a moment. All this we do and make no demur about it. That's what faith is. It is utter dependence upon and complete confidence in God.

Our biggest danger is not that we shall regard Jesus Christ as untrue but that we shall regard Him as unnecessary, that we shall trust ourselves instead of trusting Him. Only as we completely trust in the Lord Jesus, utterly depend upon Him, do we become strong against the temptations of Satan.

The last piece of defensive equipment to be named is "the helmet of salvation" (v. 17). The purpose of a helmet is to protect the head, the mind, the intelligence of man. Since Paul was addressing Christians, the reference must be to the consciousness of salvation and the protection that such consciousness gives.

I have already pointed out that doubt is one of Satan's greatest weapons. He tried to use it on the Lord Jesus, and he uses it on us. In the wilderness temptation, he went to our blessed Lord with a doubt, "If thou be the Son of God . . ." (Matt. 4:3-6). He said it twice. "If thou be the Son of God, command that these stones to be made bread." "If thou be the Son of God, cast thyself down."

If Satan can get us to doubt our relationship to God, he has us at a distinct disadvantage. This is the way the devil always moves when he comes to tempt us. He causes us to doubt our relationship to our Lord.

Many Christians are living miserable, frustrated lives because they have no assurance of their salvation. It is normal for the first thrill and joy of salvation to fade after a while. It is normal for the newness to wear off and for us to begin to wonder if we were really saved. If Satan can keep us unsure, he keeps us unhappy and useless.

Assurance is the birthright of every believer (1 John 5:13). If we know that we are saved, we have a strong defense against Satan. But if he can get us to doubt and despair, he can get us to act independent of God. Assurance then is not a luxury; it is a necessity.

What are the grounds of our assurance? There are three: the external, the internal, and the eternal. The *external evidence* is love. "By this shall all men know that ye are my disciples, if ye have love one to another" (John

13:35). The *internal evidence* is the witness of the Spirit. "The Spirit itself beareth witness with our spirit, that we are the children of God" (Rom. 8:16). The *eternal evidence* is the Word of God. God has told us plainly in the Scriptures how to be saved. If we have done what He said, the assurance of our salvation rests on that sure word from God.

God generates faith. Satan promotes uncertainty. If you've accepted Christ as your personal Savior but lack the assurance of salvation, you can be sure that your recurring doubts do not come from the Holy Spirit. His ministry is to witness with your spirit that you belong to God (Rom. 8:16). The evil one tries to hinder this work by getting you to focus on your feelings rather than on facts.

Trust that sure word from God, not your feelings. As the Social Security agent said to an applicant, "Just feeling sixty-five is not sufficient. You must be sixty-five."

Dusty Bibles and Dirty Lives

"The sword of the spirit which is the word of God" (Eph. 6:17) is the only offensive weapon in our Christian equipment, and no other is needed. With it Christians can put Satan to flight, and we find it more than adequate to meet our needs.

The use our Lord made of the written Word in His wilderness temptation lends strong support to the view that the primary and abiding application of Paul's phrase must be to the believer using the Scriptures as a mighty weapon in the conflict with evil. In the wilderness experience Jesus met every temptation with a Scripture quotation.

We cannot withstand Satan in our own wisdom or our own strength. He is wiser and stronger than we. Plus, he has had thousands of years of experience in dealing with people. Our only safe defense is the use of the Word of God. Christian experience confirms this.

A dusty Bible and a dirty life go together. Sin dulls our appetite for the Word of God, and we become weakened spiritually. The psalmist said, "Thy word have I hid in mine heart, that I might not sin against thee" (Ps. 119:11). We must discipline ourselves to a daily study of God's Word. That is never easy. Because of our busy schedules, we have trouble carving out time to study the Word of God. Satan opposes us even in that. Jesus in the parable of the sower told of the seed that was planted on the hard ground being snatched away by the birds. He identified the seed as the Word of God and the birds as Satan. He is constantly trying to snatch God's Word from our minds lest it take root and bear fruit in our lives. (Matt. 13:19).

We also learn from the wilderness temptation experience that Satan is not beyond using the Word of God. In every case in which he uses it, he either quotes only a part of it or gives a meaning to the words that does not belong to them. But Christ determined not to disobey the Scripture, and He used His knowledge of Scripture as a weapon against Satan.

The Word of God stored up in our minds is our best defensive weapon against Satan, as well as our only offensive one.

Praying All the While

While this spiritual warfare is going on, we are to be praying. Prayer is where the spiritual battle is won or lost. Jesus prayed in "agony" (Luke 22:44). The word translated "agony" is "conflict" or "struggle." In the spiritual battle we go forward best on our knees.

Paul said that prayers are to be all-inclusive. We are to pray in all ways and at all times, with all diligence for all people (Eph. 6:18). There is no substitute for prayer. We cannot make up for a failure in our devotional life by redoubling our efforts in service. So often we organize Bible studies, participate in outreach, and promote stewardship, and neglect the most vital part of our Christian experience—prayer. In our spiritual life we never can rise above what we are in our prayer life. Prayerlessness is the rankest kind of humanism.

What is prayer? Prayer is not a clever way of using divine energy for our own ends. Prayer is a way of discovering what God wants in fitting ourselves into His pattern.

We can never defeat Satan, but we can hold our ground against him. We can resist him successfully. After Satan had tried every kind of temptation on Jesus, he departed from him for a "season" (Luke 4:13). The word "season" means an opportune time. Satan's departure was not permanent. He would come again at a more opportune time. Jesus' victory over Satan was never final as long as He lived on the earth and ours will not be either.

If we want to win against Satan, we must make a sincere and honest commitment to the Lord Jesus, live holy lives, believe the gospel of peace and be ready to share it with others, live in utter dependence on the Lord, be sure of our salvation, and have a working knowledge of the Scriptures. Then, by continually praying, we can be victors instead of victims.

11

Seven Secrets to Starting Over

Recently a friend told me that her little son, Steven, came to her wanting to become a Christian. After she told him how to be saved, he prayed to receive Christ. Later that day he and his younger brother got into a fight. Steven came back into the house heartbroken and said to her in utter despair, "Oh, Mother, I just can't live the Christian life."

While most of us don't have the experience quite as soon as Steven did, we do learn quickly that failure is common in the Christian life. That should come as no surprise to us. The symbol of the Christian faith is not a cushion but a cross. The way of the Lord is the way of spiritual warfare, and we should expect a stiff fight when we begin to follow Him. Failures and disappointments are commonplace. Satan will do his best to see to that. That is a part of his work.

Satan is referred to in many ways in Scripture. He is called the accuser, the tempter, the deceiver, the murderer, the divider, the hinderer. Now I want to show you that he is the sifter or the separator.

Jesus gave us this picture of Satan when He said, "Simon, Simon, behold, Satan hath desired to have you, that he may sift you as wheat: But I have prayed for thee, that thy faith fail not: and when thou art converted, strengthen thy brethren" (Luke 22:31-32).

In these verses, Jesus made three important points. First, He told what Satan wants to do to us: He desires to "sift" us. Satan has great power, but he is not omnipotent. He can do nothing without the permission of the Lord. He has requested permission and permission has been granted. Sifting alludes to the winnowing process used by farmers to separate grain from husks. Satan's desire is ever and always the same: to shake us so as to separate us from our faith in the Lord.

Second, Jesus stated what the Lord does for us. "I have prayed for thee that thy faith fail not." The life which we have entered into is a life of faith. Our faith will be strained. This is always the point of the enemy's attack. This is the one point we must guard at all cost, no matter what may come. Satan's one aim is to shake our faith in God.

Don't let anyone ever tell you that, if you love the Lord and walk with Him, He will build a hedge of protection around you from Satan. He will not! Jesus prays for us that we will remain faithful, but He will not prevent temptation. An untested faith is no faith at all. He will allow the testing to come, but He will pray for us all the while.

Third, Jesus said what the Lord expects of us. "When thou art converted, strengthen thy brethren." He expects us to use our experience to help strengthen other believers. There is a stewardship of all of life—our experiences as well as our possessions and our talents. Though He had prayed for Peter, obviously Jesus knew that he would fail. But that would not be the end of Peter's usefulness to God. Peter was to use even his failure as a means of encouraging and helping others.

Peter refused to believe that he would fail the Lord.

"Lord, I am ready to go with thee, both into prison and to death" (v. 33). But within a few short hours, Peter learned what all of us need to know: The Lord knows us better than we know ourselves.

Jesus warned Peter that before the rooster crowed he would deny him three times. Jesus and His disciples then went from the upper room to the garden of Gethsemane. While Jesus was in prayer, the soldiers came to arrest Him. The self-willed, determined Peter drew his sword and cut off the arresting officer's ear. If he had not had such a bad aim, it would have been his head; that's what he was aiming for.

Jesus was taken to the courtyard of the high priest where He went through the mockery of a trial. Peter followed from a distance and warmed himself by an open fire as he watched and listened to the proceedings. Peter should never have been there. He was clearly in the wrong place with the wrong people. He was headed for trouble. Before long someone recognized him and asked if he weren't a friend of Jesus. He flatly denied it. Before the night was over, he had denied the Lord three times, just as Jesus said he would.

A few days later Peter went back to his old trade of fishing and influenced the other disciples to join him. He not only denied the Lord but also quit the ministry and went back to his old work.

But, thanks be to God, the story of Simon Peter does not end in failure. After Peter had denied Jesus the third time, Jesus had turned and looked at him. That look had pierced Peter's heart like a dagger and he had gone out and wept bitter tears of repentance and remorse. That was the beginning of his recovery and return. Later he met Jesus by the Sea of Galilee, and they talked. Jesus drew from Peter a threefold confession of love and devotion. Then He reassigned to his original calling the preacher who had quit.

Peter started over. Even after having cursed and denied the Lord and after having left the ministry, he was given a second chance. This is the same man who preached on the Day of Pentecost when three thousand people were saved. This is the same man who wrote two books of the New Testament. Today thousands of people proudly bear his name. He started over and made it!

There are two great lessons in Peter's experience for us today. One is that the best of men sometimes do the worst of things. Peter was one of the Lord's best men, but he denied the Lord. The difference between the saint and sinner is not sin. All human beings sin. The basic attitude toward sin makes the difference. The saint lapses into sin and loathes it. The sinner leaps into sin and loves it.

One of the marks of a true Christian is that he feels dirty when he has sinned. David was a man after God's own heart, yet he sinned grievously. In his prayer of repentance, he cried out, "Wash me thoroughly from mine iniquity, and cleanse me from my sin" (Ps. 51:2).

Being a Christian doesn't mean you won't sin. It does mean you won't enjoy it anymore. If you have been born again, you will not knowingly want to live in sin. That is because of the new nature that has been placed in you.

This truth can be illustrated by the difference between a hog and a sheep. A sheep may fall into the mud, but it hates it and scrambles out. A hog loves the mud and wallows in it. If you fall into sin and you are one of God's sheep, you will get out. If you are a hog, you will stay there and wallow in it.

The second thing Peter's experience teaches us is that failure does not have to be final. While failure is a jarring experience and can rock us on our heels, it doesn't have to be fatal. As Satan tried to shake Peter from his faith, so he will try to shake us. We can start over again and be useful once more. So, when we, like Peter, fail, we don't have to throw in the towel and quit. If the cowardly, cursing, quitting Simon Peter could start over, we can also.

If we are to be successful, we need to know how to start over again. How can Christians who fall into sin start over? When we fail, what can we do? I offer seven secrets for starting over.

Admit It, then Quit It

The first step to starting over is to make a clean break with sin. Both the Bible and human experience teach us that there are numerous ways to sin.

These are sins of temperament: anger, wrath, malice, and so forth. There are sins of the flesh: drunkenness, adultery, and other attempts to satisfy our unregenerate desires.

There are also social sins: some people who would never commit adultery are bigoted and prejudiced toward others.

And there are sins of omission. In a Bible class for young children, a pastor asked, "What do we mean by sins of omission?" Little Mary raised her hand and answered, "Those are the sins we should have committed, but didn't." That's not exactly right. Sins of omission are failing to do what we ought to do. Some people live in the world and become absorbed in its affairs without any relationship to or thought of God. They just leave God out. That is the sin of omission.

We need to see sin as anything that separates us from God or that separates us from our fellowman. It may be a sin of the temperament or a sin of the flesh. It may be what we do or what we fail to do. It matters not which. It is a sin if it separates us from God or if it separates us from our fellowman.

To start over again we must make a clean break with that sin, whatever it is. The Lord has made provision in advance for our continual forgiveness and cleansing. We are told in 1 John 1:9, "If we confess our sins, he is faithful and just to forgive us our sins, and to cleanse us from all unrighteousness." This is a promise of complete forgiveness and cleansing with a condition. The condition is that we must confess our sins. The word *confess* means "to agree with."

God accuses us of sin in two places—in the Bible and in our own conscience. When the conviction of sin comes and we confess our sins, we are agreeing with God. We are saying, "God, what you have said about me in Scripture and in my own heart is correct. You are right, I am wrong!" Confession involves seeing our lives from God's point of view.

To confess our sins is to take full responsibility for our actions. Our ability to avoid blame and excuse ourselves is frightening. It began in Eden when God asked Adam, "Have you eaten of the tree of which I commanded you not to eat?"

Adam could have said, "Yes, Lord, I did." But instead he replied, "The woman whom thou gavest to be with me, she gave me fruit of the tree." Then he lamely added, "and I ate" (Gen. 3:11-12, RSV). And when God cornered Eve and asked her about it, she said, "The serpent beguiled me, and I did eat" (v. 13). Neither was willing to accept responsibility for what they had done.

We often do the same thing. When immorality looms large in us, we conveniently say with Flip Wilson, "The devil made me do it." No! The devil didn't make you do it. The devil can tempt; he can't force. We are responsible. Yes, Pogo, you are correct: "We have met the enemy, and they is us."

Confession also implies a willingness to turn from our sin. Too many of us want God to forgive our sins without our forsaking them. That can never be. The only way to have full and free pardon of our sins is to first own and then disown them. (Prov. 28:13). We must first admit them and then quit them.

When Guilt Lingers

The second secret to beginning over is to live by faith and not by feelings. Long after our sins have been confessed and cleansed by the redemptive work of Christ, we may still have lingering guilt. When that happens, we need to remember that Satan "accused them both day and night" (Rev. 12:10). He is anxious to produce those feelings of guilt in us because they shame us and mock God.

When God forgives, He forgets. If after we have honestly and sincerely confessed a sin and turned from it and it comes to our minds again, the devil, not God, is bringing it up. Satan does not want us to remember that we are forgiven. He wants us to dwell on our failures instead of God's forgiveness. In that way he will keep you from enjoying the Christian life and being useful in God's service. So, do not depend on your feelings. God often forgives our sins long before we forgive ourselves. The ground of our assurance is God's Word, not our feelings.

The way to deal with lingering guilt is to let it be a springboard to the cross. When Satan brings to mind a sin that has been confessed and forsaken, don't dwell on your sin, feeling guilty about it. Go immediately to the cross and thank God for His forgiving mercy and grace. If you will let the memory of sin drive you to the cross instead of to despair, you will soon win the victory.

If we confess our sins to God honestly and sincerely, He forgives them and forgets them; so should we.

The Zacchaeus Principle

The third secret to starting over is to make restitution whenever possible. Do like Zacchaeus, who gave evidence of his new-found faith and genuine repentance by giving back what he had taken falsely. If you have stolen something, return it. If you have lied, correct the falsehood. If you have hurt someone, apologize. Do whatever you can to rectify the wrong that you have done so long as it does not do more harm than good.

David messed up his life with two major sins. First, with Bath-sheba he committed adultery, a passion of the moment. Then he commited a deliberate, calculated sin by having Bath-sheba's husband murdered. In both cases David committed sins where there could be no restitution. He could do nothing to bring back Bath-sheba's purity, and he could not cause Uriah to arise from the dead and be reconciled to his wife. That ugly trail of adultery and murder could never be straightened out.

In such cases we can only confess and forsake our sin and then forget those things which are behind (Phil. 3:13). If David could go from failure to forgiveness, from a messy trail to a new beginning, so can we.

The Stewardship of Experience

The fourth secret to starting over is to use your experience to help others. One of the most remarkable things about the whole story of Peter's denial and failure is his absolute honesty in the telling of it. If ever there were an incident which one might expect to be hushed up, this was it. Yet the story is told in all of its stark shame in the New Testament. The most remarkable part of it is that the story must go back to Peter himself, for no one else was there to have told it. He wanted us to know that his boast had proved vain and that Jesus' prediction had come true. He wanted us to know that his faith had failed under the pressure of temptation.

Peter made this incident an essential part of his preaching and did so for the very best reason. Everytime he told the story, he could say, "Look at me. Look what I did. And still Jesus forgave me. He forgave me when I failed Him in His bitterest hour of need. He took me, Peter, the coward and quitter, and used even me. What Jesus did for me, He can surely do for you."

This was a practical working out of what Jesus had told Peter to do, "When thou art converted, strengthen thy brethren." It is often out of our failures that we give our greatest testimony.

Don't Run with Dogs

The fifth secret to starting over is go to the right places and associate with the right people. A big part of Peter's problem to begin with was being at the wrong place with the wrong people. He should never have been at the trial of Jesus. He should never have warmed himself by the enemy's campfire. He overmatched himself and wound up denying his Lord.

That's a danger we all face. We can't travel the fast lane of life and associate with swingers without winding up out of breath and dizzy. Friends exert a tremendous influence upon us. Sam Jones was right when he said, "You can't run with dogs without getting fleas on you."

We should never underestimate our adversaries. Evil men make bad friends and bad places are breeding grounds for trouble we don't need. Do not be deceived: "Bad company ruins good morals" (1 Cor. 15:33, RSV).

Growing in Grace or Disgrace

The sixth secret for starting over is to keep on the growing edge of life. Some people climb so far in the Christian life and then settle down so hard they flatten out. We should never stop growing.

We must give special attention to inner strength. We are body, soul, and spirit. We are one-third physical and two-thirds spiritual. Therefore, our greatest needs are spiritual. Far too many people attempting to start over, overstuff their body and starve their soul.

We are vain, conceited, self-centered people. We make up, paint up, and dress up our bodies, but neglect our spiritual lives. We are instructed by Peter to "grow in grace and in the knowledge of our Lord and Saviour Jesus Christ" (2 Pet. 3:18). We are not to stay as we are. We are born to grow. Growth is natural for the Christian. Stagnation, standing still, is abnormal. The fact is, we either grow in grace or we grow in disgrace.

He Gives Both the Will and the Ability

Here is the seventh secret to starting over: Don't try to make it on your own. Why? Because you can't and because you don't have to! You are not alone. At the very moment you committed your life to Christ, you received the gift of the Holy Spirit. It is His indwelling presence that can give you victory.

Paul told the Philippians that salvation is a free gift of God that comes to us through faith in Christ. However, we are to carry it to completion, to its full potential. How are we to do that? "It is God which worketh in you both to will and to do his good pleasure" (Phil. 2:13). He gives us both the desire and the ability to fulfill His glorious purpose for our life. If there is a desire in our hearts to serve God, it was put there by the Lord. The same one who gave us the desire will also give us the ability. He will enable us to overcome our problems and the attacks of Satan.

So, you see, you are not on your own. You have all the power of heaven at your disposal. And the Holy Spirit will never disappoint you. He you desperately need and can definitely depend on all the time. You can, if it is His will, make it with no human help. But you cannot make it without the power, comfort, guidance, and teaching of the Holy Spirit.

Anyone who reads these lines can start over and make it if he really wants to. Peter came back from failure to usefulness and you can too.

Tucked away in Jeremiah 18 is a wonderful object lesson. The prophet said, "Then I went down to the potter's house, and behold he wrought a work on the wheels. And the vessel that he made was marred in the hand of the potter: so he made it again another vessel, as seemed good to the potter to make it" (vv. 3-4).

The potter in the object lesson is God. We are the clay—the people of God. The clay is in the hand of the potter even as we are in the hands of God. God is seeking to mold our lives into vessels of honor. At some point in the molding and shaping process, a flaw or crack may become visible. It is ugly and makes the vessel useless. The crack may be a crime committed against society, an act of adultery, a blazing temper, an act of violence, a divorce, or even child abuse. It is ugly! The potter could crush the piece of clay and throw it into the garbage heap. He is the potter, he can do what he wills. But instead, the potter molds the piece of clay into another vessel, a useful vessel, a vessel of honor.

That is what God wants to do with your broken, bent, twisted, confused, cracked life. Place yourself in the wonderful hands of Jesus the Potter and let Him start over on the clay of your life today.

12

The Downfall of the Great Deceiver

At the end of every heart-tugging sermon, an old backslider made his way to the altar and prayed, "Lord, remove the cobwebs of sin from my heart."

Every week the backslider went through the same procedure. Finally, a godly brother joined him at the altar. He listened to the backslider's usual prayer and added earnestly, "Lord, forget about those cobwebs; just get rid of the spider!"

The only hope any of us has of living without the continual confession of and cleansing from sin is the removal of its source—Satan. This has been our hope from the very beginning.

Sin entered the world when Adam and Eve yielded to Satan's temptation in the Garden. At that time Satan became the god of this world, dominating it by sin and death. But even in the Garden God promised redemption. He said to Satan, "I will put enmity [hostility]/Between you and the woman,/And between your seed and her seed;/He shall bruise you on the head,/And you shall bruise him on the heel" (Gen. 3:15, NASB). This familiar verse promised the coming of the Lord Jesus Christ and His victory over Satan. The seed of the woman was to trample on the head of the devil.

On the cross Jesus was bruised by the power of sin and Satan, but there He also crushed Satan. The ultimate defeat of Satan was accomplished.

By now we have looked at Satan in almost every aspect of his work. We have seen him as the accuser, the tempter, the deceiver, the divider, the hinderer, the afflictor, and the sifter. Now I want to show him as the loser. He is a defeated foe.

A Dethroned Prince

From the outset of his ministry, Jesus was engaged in a life-and-death conflict with Satan and his demons. We find a testimony of this fact in the response of demons to our Lord. Matthew 8:28 records that Christ crossed the Sea of Galilee to the country of the Gergesenes; there he "met two possessed with devils, coming out of the tombs, exceeding fierce, so that no man might pass by that way." When demons saw the Lord Jesus Christ, "they cried out, saying, What have we to do with thee, Jesus, thou Son of God? art thou come hither to torment us before the time?"

The demons recognized that they were under judgment. They also recognized that Jesus Christ was the Judge and that by the word of His mouth a predetermined judgment would be meted out upon them; the sentence passed would be executed. They also knew something of the program of God and the time that it would take place, for when Jesus comes to the earth to reign, the first demonstration of His sovereign authority over the earth will be to bind Satan and to remove him from this sphere.

They knew then that their judgment and the coming of Christ to reign would coincide. Since Jesus was rejected by Israel at His first advent, they were smart enough to

The Downfall of the Great Deceiver

deduce that the time of this judgment had not arrived, even though the Judge was personally present. Jesus cast the demons out of the men, and the men were set free from Satan's control.

According to Luke 10:10-18, Jesus had sent out the seventy on a preaching mission, and they came back with glowing reports of success. They said, "Lord, even the demons are subject to us in your name" (v. 17, RSV) In response Jesus said, "I beheld Satan as lightning fall from heaven" (v. 18)

The demons represent Satan's power on earth. In their defeat Jesus foresaw the final defeat of Satan and the ultimate triumph of the kingdom of God. He saw in the preaching of the seventy the power of Satan being broken. He saw this as an evidence of the sudden, complete, and decisive defeat of Satan. As the disciples gave their report, Jesus remembered the prophecy of Genesis 3:15, anticipated His coming crucifixion and resurrection, and saw that through the preaching of the good news the final defeat of Satan would be accomplished.

Later, in John 12, our Lord announced to the disciples the certainty of His victory. In a prophetic revelation, He said that Satan was a vanquished foe. After our Lord had spoken of His death on the cross, likening that death to a kernel of wheat falling onto the ground to die so that it might bring forth the great harvest, He said, "Now is the judgment of this world; now shall the prince of this world be cast out" (v. 31).

After having spoken of His death, He next spoke of His resurrection. He said, "I, if I be lifted up from the earth, will draw all men unto me" (v. 32). He was speaking of the resurrection in which, by the Spirit of God, He would be lifted up from the grave, from the power of death and the power of Satan, and exalted to the right hand of God. And

He promised that when He was lifted up He would draw all men unto Him. Even from among those who had been drawn to Satan, our Lord said there will be those drawn to Him, for He is the victor over Satan.

Jesus saw the cross as a struggle between good and evil, light and darkness, God and Satan, two rulers contending for world supremacy. But He also saw Satan as losing. He would be cast down and defeated. Since Eden Satan had ruled people by sin and death. Through His crucifixion Christ conquered sin. Through His resurrection He conquered death. He triumphed over sin at the cross and over death at the empty tomb. So, at this time, Jesus heralded the fact that Satan had been judged. The execution of final judgment is only a matter of time.

After his defeat by England at the Battle of Waterloo, Napoleon was exiled to the island of Saint Helena. One day he was poring over a map of Europe that had the British Isles outlined in red. As his finger rested on that spot, he was heard to mutter to himself, "If it had not been for that red spot, I'd have conquered the world."

Satan must be saying something similar today. Were it not for the red spot of Calvary in the history of the world, the victory over man would have been his. But, thanks be to God, there is victory over sin and death because of Jesus' death on the cross and resurrection from the tomb.

The death of Christ was the means and the cross of Christ was the place of judgment upon Satan. The adversary, who had begun his rebellion against God before the creation of the world, was now brought before the bar of judgment. By his death and resurrection Jesus passed sentence upon the adversary of God.

The simple truth of these verses is that Satan was defeated on the cross. He is now a deposed, dethroned ruler.

A Disarmed Adversary

Satan is a defeated foe but not a dead one. He has been dethroned, but he has not been destroyed. He is still alive and active. Satan's defeat did not remove him from the picture. He is still very much with us.

The Bible makes it clear that, while Satan has already been judged, condemned to the pit of hell, he will continue to work until he enters the age when his final overthrow is complete.

Emil Brunner put it this way, "The most important truth about the devil is this: Jesus Christ has conquered him. It is equally true that the devil is active and is endeavoring to keep men from entering into the power of that conquest."

Recently I visited with Betty Welch, a Wycliffe Bible translator who works among the Tucano Indians of Colombia, South America. She told me that last year Wycliffe translators worked among forty-one Indian tribes in Colombia. Now, for security reasons, only seven translators are among the tribes. The guerrilla warfare has made it too dangerous. She said, "We are nearing the completion of the translation and publication of the New Testament in the Tucano language, and the nearer we get to the completion of the project the more opposition we seem to have, either in the form of guerrilla fighting or government regulations." Betty continued, "It is obviously the work of Satan who does not want to see the Word of God placed in the hands of the people. He is the great hinderer to the work of God.

"When we are translating the parts of the New Testament that have to do with Satan, we seem to have many more problems than any other time. The translation of the language is much more difficult, and fellow missionaries in translation meetings are edgier and flare up quicker at one another. Apparently Satan doesn't want people to know what he's really like.

"We have learned," Betty went on, "to expect that kind of opposition, and we now encourage and enlist people to join us in special prayer during such times."

I had just begun a series of sermons on Satan at the time we talked, and so Betty warned, "You need to enlist people to pray for you also during this series. Satan will be attacking you more severely than ever before."

You know what? Betty was right. Never in any period in my ministry have I been more attacked than during the past few months.

Even though Satan is still active, he no longer has dominion over us. The writer of Hebrews declared, "Forasmuch then as the children are partakers of flesh and blood, he also himself likewise took part of the same; that through death he might destroy him that had the power of death, that is, the devil" (Heb. 2:14).

The word which is translated "destroy" is the Greek word *katargeo*. It literally means "to make of none effect." The devil has not been destroyed in the sense of being done away with, a fact which is obvious. What has happened to him is even more thrilling than the thought of his being abolished completely from existence. He has been stripped of his power, disarmed, as well as dethroned.

In order to get the full impact of the meaning of *katargeo*, and thus the disposition of Satan because of Calvary, we need to look briefly at some other references involving the use of this same Greek word.

Paul wrote to Timothy, "But [the grace of God] is now made manifest by the appearing of our Savior Jesus Christ, who hath abolished [*Katargeo*] death and hath brought life and immortality to light through the gospel" (2 Tim. 1:10). What Jesus did to death, He did to Satan.

In the parable of the barren fig tree, Luke wrote, "Then said he to the dresser of his vineyard, Behold, these three years I come seeking fruit on this fig tree, and find none; cut it down; why cumbereth [*katargeo*] it the ground?" (Luke 13:7). What the fig tree did to the ground, rendering it useless, Jesus did to Satan.

Through the amazing mystery of the cross and the resurrection, Jesus has broken the power and bondage of Satan over human lives. Those who individually receive and acknowledge Him are set free to live in the freedom and liberty of the children of God. As John declared, "For this purpose the Son of God was manifested, that he might destroy the works of the devil" (1 John 3:8).

Jesus has "loosed" us from the bondage of sin and Satan. Our Savior stripped Satan of his power so that he is actually powerless against Christians who trust the Lord in spiritual warfare.

Without a doubt, the evil one thought he had conquered when Christ died, but the real truth is that Satan was overcome by virtue of that death, and the believer also can, by virtue of it, defy all the powers of Satan and set them at naught.

Now the devil can never totally defeat the Christian. Those who are genuinely the Lord's, who are born again and have come into a saving relationship with Jesus Christ, are delivered from total defeat. We do not hesitate to emphasize that! The devil can never get us back into the position of unconscious control which he once exercised over us and which he exercises over the rest of the world.

Sin no longer has to dominate our lives. It will not be the habit of our lives if we are Jesus'. Habitual actions are an index to character. This does not mean that the Christian will never commit an act of sin, rather, he will not make sin the ruling principle of his life. It is possible to live victoriously because Jesus has disarmed as well as dethroned the enemy. Therefore, he can never totally defeat us. We are never alone. He gives us immediate help and ultimate victory.

A Doomed Enemy

Dethroned, disarmed, doomed! What a tragic end for one who had such a brilliant beginning.

The writer of Revelation predicted the final and complete doom of Satan. When Christ shall return to the Mount of Olives at the end of the age, an angel will bind Satan for a thousand years. At the close of that millennium, Satan will then be loosed for a season to deceive the nations. Then God will cast Satan and his followers into the lake of fire where he will be tormented day and night forever and forever (Rev. 20:1-3, 7-10).

In Revelation 20 we have a description of the initial phase of the execution of the predetermined judgment of God on Satan. We read in Revelations 19:11-16 of the second advent of Jesus Christ to the earth where He comes as a victor, pictured as riding on a white horse. He bears the name King of kings and Lord of lords. And after subjugating nations that are in rebellion against Him at His second advent (v. 15), we read in Revelation 20:1-3: "I saw an angel come down from heaven, having the key to the bottomless pit and a great chain in his hand. And he laid hold on the dragon, that old serpent, which is the Devil, and Satan, and bound him a thousand years, And cast him into the bottomless pit, and shut him up, and set a seal upon him, that he should deceive the nations no more, till the thousand years should be fulfilled."

The Downfall of the Great Deceiver

Satan's opposition has prevented the reign of the Lord Jesus Christ over the earth and the institution of the literal kingdom of God upon the earth. People have a fallen, sinful nature. Satan can still deceive people, even the saints of God. Satan can pervert them from the path of obedience to God, distort their affections, and turn them aside from the love of God, and can blind their minds to the truth of God. Satan is active in his work of deception to prevent the reign of Christ over this earth in that age we know as the millenial age.

When Jesus comes to fulfill the purpose and the program of God to reign from sea to sea and from shore to shore, He will remove our adversary the devil, the deceiver, from the scene. Christ will bind Satan and seal him in a bottomless pit so that he cannot come forth during the time of our Lord's earthly reign to deceive the nations. And this earth will experience a reign of righteousness.

The binding of Satan is a sign to all heaven and to earth that Jesus Christ actually is King of kings and Lord of lords. God has authenticated Jesus Christ as the one who is the Son of God by the resurrection from the dead. The resurrection is evidence to us that Jesus is Savior and Lord. But God will give another demonstration of the authority of Christ at the second advent. That demonstration is the binding and removing of Satan. The vast majority of miracles recorded in the Gospels are in the realm of demonism, miracles dealing with deliverance of people who were blind, deaf, or dumb because they were possessed by Satan's demons. These were evidence that the authority of Christ exceeded the authority of Satan, for Christ could go into Satan's realm and remove those who were in bondage and grant them deliverance. It is a picture of what Christ will do when He comes the second time to reign.

Not only will Satan be removed but also all the demons who were subservient to him so that for the first time since the fall of Adam the world will be without demonic influences. The reason the earth can blossom as a rose is that it will not be blighted by Satan's weeds. The reason men can live in righteousness and justice and peace is that the inhabitants will not be blighted by Satan's lies. Jesus Christ will reign as King of kings and Lords of lords from sea to sea, because He has bound Satan.

But that is only the first step toward the final destiny of Satan. We read in Revelation 20:3 that after the thousand years Satan must be loosed for a little season. Then the activity of Satan in the brief period in which he is loosed is described in verses 7-9. He goes forth to do what he was prevented from doing during the thousand years of Christ's earthly reign. He goes forth to deceive the nations, and that which once worked so well is attempted again. Satan repeats his previous sin and goes forth to deceive the nations, to offer himself as their king, and to promise that, if they follow him, he will deliver them from the obligation of being in subjection to Jesus Christ. Those who were rebels against Christ now for the first time are able to join in rebellion against Him. They flock to the one whom they delight to acknowledge as their lord and their master and trust that he will deliver them from judgment by dethroning the Judge who reigns, even the Lord Jesus Christ. After this new flurry of activity, we read in verse 10 of Satan's doom. The devil that deceived them is cast into the lake of fire and brimstone, where the beast and the false prophet are, and shall be tormented day and night forever and forever.

The devil may rage as a roaring lion now and throughout history, but the Bible reveals that his ultimate fate is to be cast into hell. With him will be all who reject and oppose Christ.

Through sentiment, not sound reason or Scripture, many say that a God of love could not create man and then condemn him to hell. The Bible says that hell was not prepared for man, but for the devil and his angels (Matt. 25:41). God has made full provision to prevent men from going to hell. But if they reject His redemption, preferring to serve the devil, then they choose to go to hell with him. So, it is by the devil's will, not God's, that man go to hell.

The word used by Jesus for hell as a place of punishment is *Gehenna*. It refers to the Valley of Hinnom which was the garbage dump of Jerusalem in Jesus' day. All filth, the bodies of dead animals, and even the unclaimed bodies of executed criminals were thrown there. Fires burned day and night to burn the filth. Maggots worked constantly in it. At night wild dogs came to feed on the edible portions. They howled and gnashed their teeth as they fought over the food.

Jesus said that this was a symbol of hell. But the reality is always greater than the symbol. Heaven is more wonderful and hell more terrible than the symbols used for them. Fire is the most awful pain known to man. Hell will be worse.

So the devil and all who follow him will be cast into hell forever at the final judgment. Those who follow Satan are destined to ultimate defeat, even as he is. Those who follow Christ will enter into heaven forever.

Borrowing from Jesus' symbol, hell may be seen as God's cosmic garbage dump. All that is not fit for heaven will be cast into the garbage dump. The earth was created to be a habitation for man, but when Adam rebelled his destiny was changed; he no longer had a right to the presence of God but joined with Satan and shared Satan's destiny. The lake of fire was not prepared for any human being. It was prepared for the devil and his angels. It becomes the destiny of men because they join Satan and his rebellion.

The lake of fire need not be your destiny, for Jesus Christ came to bring you to God by offering Himself as a sacrifice for the sin of the world. No salvation was provided for angels, for those who sinned with Satan were destined for the lake of fire with no hope or promise of salvation whatsoever. But God, in grace, has offered salvation to you. The decision is yours: heaven or the lake of fire—Jesus Christ or Satan. Which will it be?

The apostle Paul, describing the glory that belonged to Jesus Christ, reminded us that when He became obedient unto death, even to death on the cross, "God also hath highly exalted him, and given him a name which is above every name: That at the name of Jesus every knee should bow, of things in heaven, and things in earth, and things under the earth; And that every tongue should confess that Jesus Christ is Lord, to the glory of God the Father" (Phil. 2:9-11).

And in the unending ages of eternity, no tongue will be lifted against the absolute authority of the Lord Jesus Christ. All heaven will confess him as glorified Lord and Savior. The unfallen angels will adore and serve him. Even those banished from His presence will confess that the king whom they loved and served was an imposter and deceiver and that Jesus Christ was the rightful Lord.

No one will rebel against Jesus' will, for all in heaven will recognize His authority and bow in obedience to Him. No other lord will invite submission, for Jesus will rule as Lord forever. To Him be glory and honor, dominion and majesty, love and praise forever!